Contents

Introduction

Bed and Breakfasts are the combination of several great loves of mine.
Those loves, being both food and traveling to unknown places. In
researching the B&B industry in America, I discovered the kindest
collection of individuals who collectively put others first. As you read
this and the other books in the America's Best Bed and Breakfast
Series, you realize that most of these entrepreneurs don't get into this
industry to become wealthy. Instead, they have a genuine love of
people despite being part of the competitive travel industry.

These owners offered tips for travelers, advice for future innkeepers,
recipes, and their stories. Most of these B&B's are privately owned and
operated and depend on their reputation and word of mouth from satisfied customers. I hope this book teaches you something you didn't
know about B&B's and inspires you to visit some of these wonderful
locations.

Jon Nelsen

ONE

The Katherine Holle House B&B

119 N Church St
Watertown, Wisconsin 53094

Keri K.

WHAT TIME DO YOU WAKE UP EACH MORNING AND WHAT DOES YOUR schedule look like?

Most of our guests eat breakfast at 8am, so we usually start at 630 making the bacon, so the yummy smell wafts upstairs and wakes everyone up!

What is the most rewarding part of the job?

The most rewarding job is having our guests tell us how comfortable their stay was, how relaxed they were and how they 'haven't slept that great in years!

Do you need to be a great cook to run a B&B?

Great? No. Creative? Sure.

Can one person run a B&B themselves? At what point do you need help?

It all depends on your organizational skills, your time allowance and your energy level. One person could, with maybe 3 rooms and 25% occupancy, but over that you really need more than one.

How do you deal with check-ins and check-outs?

We greet our guests at the door, show them their rooms and explain everything. We give them an access code, to let themselves in and out as they wish, and they checkout after breakfast in the morning.

TWO

Greenbriar Inn

315 E Wallace Ave,
Coeur d'Alene, ID 83814

Kris McILvenna

WHAT TIME DO YOU WAKE UP EACH MORNING AND WHAT DOES YOUR schedule look like?

I get up at 6:00, and am at work by 7:00. Because we have a restaurant, I am usually here until at least 6:00 PM. Sometimes later.

What is the most rewarding part of the job?

There is immediate gratification in this job. People thank us profusely for the great experience.

Do you need to be a great cook to run a B&B?

Not great, but be interested in what your customers are requesting, and modify it to suit your needs. There are plenty of great cooking tutorials and ideas on the internet.

Can one person run a B&B themselves? At what point do you need help?

If it were a one or two bedroom, I'm sure. But when you have more rooms than that, you'll need some help.

How do you deal with check-ins and check-outs?

Everyone that checks in has a key to the front door so they can come and go as they please. We give people a little extra time if they need it for check outs.

THREE

1899 Inn Deadwood

21 Lincoln Avenue,
Deadwood, South Dakota 57732

Nyla Griffith
Innkeeper

WHAT TIME DO YOU WAKE UP EACH MORNING AND WHAT DOES YOUR schedule look like?

I am up at 5:30am every day of the week and work making and serving breakfast until about 10am, I start the homemade sourdough bread so it can rise and be turned all day, then we start cleaning the rooms. I may take some time to do paperwork, register reservations that came in overnight, etc. in between serving guests, which happens in three seatings. Check-ins start at 2pm and run through 9pm but I usually have some time to sit down and make a dinner for Tom and myself during that time. Breakfast for the next day is prepped between 2pm and 6pm. Most people call with questions and asking for reservations between 6pm and 9pm.

What is the most rewarding part of the job?

Seeing the success of the business and a return on all of your hard work. The great reviews always warm my heart. Many people don't mention it to us in person but in the review they will tell us how their stay has changed their lives or how happy they were. It is such a pleasure to read their words.

Do you need to be a great cook to run a B&B?

Yes. No question. Or hire one but it will never be the same as doing it yourself.

Can one person run a B&B themselves? At what point do you need help?

Maybe but it's very difficult once you pass four rooms.

How do you deal with check-ins and check-outs?

One at a time. Each person is special and have special needs.
You talk to everyone of them and help them with dinner
reservations, planning their day trips, and a personal tour of the
Inn. Check-outs are also personal with a huge "thank you" and
making sure they have your number for the next stay.

FOUR

Rabbit Hill Inn

48 Lower Waterford Rd
Lower Waterford, Vermont, 05848

Brian & Leslie Mulcahy
Innkeepers

2020 Travel+Leisure #1 Best Resort Hotel in the Northeast

#3 Best Hotel in the USA / #39 Best Hotel in the World

Over the 27 years of our innkeeping life, we've earned several awards and distinctions. Most recently, we are very proud and humbled to have been named #1 Hotel in the Northeast, #3 Hotel in the US, and #39 Hotel in the world in Travel+Leisure Magazine's World's Best Awards. We have appeared on this list several times; but for the past two years, we've taken the #1 spot for the Northeast. What is especially great about this is the company that we're in. This "mom & pop" inn in Lower Waterford, Vermont has taken the lead over properties across the world who charge thousands of dollars per night and have marketing teams that spend more in a day what we might spend in two years.

...a deliciously romantic
Vermont experience!

WHAT TIME DO YOU WAKE UP EACH MORNING AND WHAT DOES YOUR schedule look like?

This question really varies with the type of property each of us operates. I personally arrive at my desk around 7:30 in the morning. But we are also a full-service inn with a staff of some 22 to 25 people. But that doesn't mean we still aren't here for 13 to 15 hours each and every day. And even if we are not physically here, we are attached by cellphone, walkie-talkie, or computer. Work goes beyond making breakfast and changing beds. There is an entire business that needs to be administered to – finance, human resources, marketing, management, maintenance, budgeting, etc.

What is the most rewarding part of the job?

Knowing that you've helped to provide a couple with an experience they may not soon forget. We cater to a romantic adult getaway. But those couples may have just lost a child or parent; they may have a relationship that's on the rocks. We play a role in helping to make them whole – in bringing peace and comfort. We can provide a distraction from the things they wish to escape; or we can provide a time to focus on the things they need to think about. But most of the time, we provide relaxation and a chance for couples to reconnect.

Do you need to be a great cook to run a B&B?

No. You just need to HIRE a good one!

Can one person run a B&B themselves? At what point do you need help?

Too many factors involved to answer this one. A very small property, one or two rooms, might be handled by one person. Five or six rooms would require at least 2 people. How much service do you wish to provide? With COVID, many properties have moved to a "touchless" model. Everything is done to avoid personal contact. Technology replaces humanity. That can work for some types of places. Would not work here.

How do you deal with check-ins and check-outs?

Just as we do with every other aspect of running the inn. We are here for our guests… from the welcome (check-in) to the good-byes (check-out).

FIVE

The Barn B&B Walla Walla

1624 Stovall Road
Walla Walla, WA 99362

Anand & Naina Rao

After just 9 months in operation we were awarded the TripAdvisor Traveler's Choice Award. We also got 3 Diamonds from AAA.

What time do you wake up each morning and what does your schedule look like?

We're up at 5:30 am. Breakfast is served at 8:30 am. By the time service is over and everything is cleaned up and put away, it's after 11 am. Then it's time for email, reservation management, menu planning with the chef and ensuring our suites are being serviced and cleaned to the highest level. During Covid, we do not enter the suite at all after guest check-in but we hope to return to normal.

What is the most rewarding part of the job?

To make people feel special and want to return

Do you need to be a great cook to run a B&B?

Not necessarily though a knowledge of food, service and what happens in the kitchen are handy. You'd need to find good help in the kitchen if you don't know too much about it. Housekeeping is also critical.

Can one person run a B&B themselves?

A lot depends on the level of service and amenities provided. 4 rooms and under, probably yes. At what point do you need help? We'd say 5 rooms and up you'd probably need some help, even part-time either in the kitchen or the rooms or both.

How do you deal with check-ins and check-outs?

Both check-in and check-out are touchless. We are on what we call 'guest watch'. Our office faces where the vehicles park. One of us is on the look-out and the guests also text us when they're about 10 minutes away. We then welcome them at their vehicle. After their welcome drink of Walla Walla wine, we used to walk them to their suite and take them on a tour of it. During Covid, we send them a YouTube video tour of the suite instead and walk them to the door of their suite and stop there.

SIX

Brass Lantern Inn

717 Maple Street
Stowe, Vermont

George Lewis

·   **Certificate of Excellence, Trip Advisor.com for multiple years of excellent guest review comments**

·   **2019 Traveler's Choice, Best B&B/Inn in the United States – top 25 B&B in the U.S. from TripAdvisor.com**

·   **2020 Stowe Business People of the Year Award – recognized by the Stowe Visitor's Center, Stowe Area Association**

WHAT TIME DO YOU WAKE UP EACH MORNING AND WHAT DOES YOUR schedule look like?

Our schedule varies dramatically from season to season. Generally, we are up by 5:30 +/- each day to prepare for breakfast service. We transition then to breakfast clean up, daily housekeeping including on-site laundry duties. We manage the marketing needs of the day, respond to e-mail requests, take care of financial management and HR needs. Building and grounds duties include mowing the grass, watering the gardens, shoveling the snow, cleaning the common areas, attending to short term repairs, plunge out a toilet to replacing a towel rod that a guest mistook as a grab bar. We then get the afternoon cookies/tea prepared, prepare the paperwork for check in arrivals (from 3 to 8). In the winter - clean out the wood stove in the common living room, reset with fresh wood, help guests make dinner reservations for the evening, etc. For long stretches of any given season we repeat this cycle daily from about 5:30 a.m. until about 8:30 in the evening every day. For our 9 guest room B&B we depend on each of us to be on full time and pre-covid we had a seasonal full time housekeeper.

With a dependable staff person, both Mary Anne and I fully committed we tend to go with the "make hay while the sunshine's" kind of deal, taking any opportunity to grab an hour or two for ourselves and then re-charge our batteries with a vacation ourselves. We have had some very profitable seasons where we have gone 12+ weeks or more without a day off. When short staffed, funny, we see a trip to the Post Office as an escape! With time and success in the business we have found that it is more productive and more enjoyable to actually schedule some down time/close the inn for a night or two. Otherwise, risk of burn out is high.

What is the most rewarding part of the job?

The guests. The fact that we get to live in this business with the most amazing lifestyle in a wonderful location. Remember, guests go out of their way to come here as their destination, vacation! And owning this type of business has the personal reward of witnessing people having a great time due to your efforts in our favorite place. Very rewarding, indeed.

Do you need to be a great cook to run a B&B?

I don't think you could be a mediocre cook and provide the unique experience that we believe most people are looking for when booking a stay at a full/real bed and breakfast kind of lodging option. We have always felt and believe it has become true that we can set ourselves apart from the completion (and yes, keep up with the competition) by elevating the experience with a truly amazing breakfast. A breakfast that our guests would love to have every day, but, ultimately thankful that they didn't have to spend the time to create this breakfast.

Can one person run a B&B themselves? At what point do you need help?

Depends on the number of rooms and the type of experience you want to provide to the guests. For a single Innkeeper, no additional staff, I wouldn't want to do more than 2 or 3 guest rooms. For our nine guest rooms, it takes both Mary Anne and I to be fully committed, this is our only source of livelihood, and a full time seasonal housekeeper (pre-covid). Fortunately, the business has grown to support this additional position. This and a part-time bookkeeper provides a manageable lifestyle. Busy and dedicated, but, not overwhelming.

How do you deal with check-ins and check-outs?

As one of the reasons for getting into this business was the opportunity to meet people and to solidify the personal level of service we personally welcome and great each guest to our Inn. The exception is for those arriving after 8 pm. where we have a secure late night check in procedure. This initial greeting is so important for us to hopefully understand the expectations of the guest, for the guests to recognize that our primary goal here is for them to have an incredible experience and set the overall tone of their stay. It's personal, they are coming to stay in our house and we want them to feel very welcome. Check out –we have this sign in our entry hall, "Arrive as our Guest and Depart as our Friend." We always take the time to provide a personal goodbye and thank you for your stay.

SEVEN

The Lion and the Rose Bed & Breakfast

276 Montford Ave,
Asheville, NC 28801

Karen & Steve Wilson

- Our gardens became a certified wildlife habitat by the National Wildlife Federation.

- We started a fun giving back project called "Inn Support of our Troops". We worked with a non-profit organization, Soldiers Angels, and rallied over 30 other inns to send home baked goodies to soldiers overseas. We plan to make this project an annual event and hope to get more inns to participate.

- In 2021, our B&B was a prize on the epic game show, The Price is Right.

WHAT TIME DO YOU WAKE UP EACH MORNING AND WHAT DOES YOUR schedule look like?

We get up around 6:30am every morning. Steve and I both have different schedules as we take on different chores but we also do occasionally mix up the responsibilities. Steve will brew a fresh pot of coffee and deliver a tray to each guest. We both will prep ingredients and double check for any special dietary requirements. Steve is in charge of breakfast and does most of the cooking. Karen will sanitize all the tables and set the places for the number of guests that particular morning. Karen will serve drinks and the two courses to all guests making sure every need is attended to. If guests have any questions, want recommendations or just want to chat, Karen is happy to accommodate those needs as well. We both work on breakfast cleanup and sanitizing the dining areas again. 11am check-out time comes around and it's time to say until we meet again. Currently, we do not have a housekeeper so we are cleaning and sanitizing all rooms and common areas. Depending on the weather, there are more afternoon chores such as gardening, lawn care, snow removal, etc. Accounting, bookkeeping, shopping, planning for the next day (or week's) menu, taking reservations, answering phone calls and other chores are done in between breakfast and check-ins or basically whenever we can squeeze them in. 3-5pm is check-in time and we welcome new guests and try our best to make them feel at home. Some days are harder and longer than others, especially weekend days. When we do have spare time, we enjoy getting out for a hike with our dogs, researching restaurants and breweries.

What is the most rewarding part of the job?

Meeting so many wonderful people and creating new friendships! We love to trade travel stories, talk about nature, the outdoors and beer.

Do you need to be a great cook to run a B&B?

Yes and no. I would say that as long as you have some type of cooking experience, you enjoy it and feel confident experimenting with new recipes, you will become a great cook in no time.

Can one person run a B&B themselves? At what point do you need help?

It depends on the size of the B&B. If it is a smaller one, I believe one person could run it themselves. Would they really want to take all the chores alone is the real question. The more rooms you have and the longer season you have, the more you would need help whether it be a housekeeper, a gardener, etc.

How do you deal with check-ins and check-outs?

Our check-in window is 3-5PM. I usually handle the check-ins when they arrive. I give them a little tour around the house to get them familiar with all the main details they need to know regarding breakfast time, dietary needs, etc. and of course, pour them a pint of beer. If a guest plans to arrive after 5PM, we have a self check-in option that gives them instructions on how to get their keys and get into the house. Check-out is very informal and simple. The keys are left in the room and we send an email receipt.

EIGHT

Cameo Heights Mansion

1072 Oasis Rd,
Touchet, WA 99360

We were voted top 10 romantic places to stay in the world (right up there with Paris!) by Bed&Breakfast.com and have also received awards from Opentable for our dining and Trip Advisor for our inn and restaurant.

WHAT TIME DO YOU WAKE UP EACH MORNING AND WHAT DOES YOUR
schedule look like?

When we first started, we were working 18 hour days because we had to do everything, not being able to afford employees. Now after 14 years, we pay a lot of people to do many of the jobs we used to do and so even though we stay busy, we can leave for extended vacations and personal hobbies. We are still very occupied when we are here. Typically we get up at 6:30 AM, once a week, I still do breakfast but other mornings I work on books putting in receipts, balancing accounts, filing reports, payroll, employee correspondence. My husband first thing writes a little newsletter with the weather, some musings for the day to send up with the fresh coffee and Danish we deliver at 8 AM to our guest on a tray to their suites. Then he heads up marketing, works on seeing the trends in our business, works on website improvements, visits with our marketing groups, handles any major maintenance issues, and always has an improvement project going viz; he made solar panels for our pool last spring, put in a new septic system, designed an outdoor eating area for covid restrictions, etc. We usually visit with guests during breakfast and during dinner in the evening and finish up around 7 pm in the evening though my husband often works later than that. We have both served on national and state and city bed and breakfast boards and committees. You really learn a lot in the industry when you work with peers. Rubbing shoulders with the best of the best is the best education you can receive.

What is the most rewarding part of the job?

Definitely the guests!!! Also, the creative energy, the dreaming and planning and finding ways to deal with problems. We also love being able to work together – at least most days!

Do you need to be a great cook to run a B&B?

Not if you can afford to hire one....

Can one person run a B&B themselves?

We know several people who run small 2 or 3 room b&b's. The size of the business is what determines the necessity of employees. If you don't want the hassle of employees, keep it small. At what point do you need help? You need help when you find yourself losing the joy of the job and you can afford to hire someone to give you some days off. Or if your investment is small, then you just shut down and take off a few days. We didn't have that luxury as our business is a restaurant and seven suites with lots of investment.

How do you deal with check-ins and check-outs?

We have innovated much since we first began. We liked having the opportunity to interact with guests so we gave them a personal check-in for years and personal check outs on the day they left. Since the pandemic, we have found a new technology that allows a personal interaction without the face to face and instead uses texting-- which our guests have loved.

NINE

The Victoria Inn Bed & Breakfast

430 High Street (Rt. 27E)
Hampton, NH 03842

Tracey Dewhurst
Proprietor

"The Seacoast's Finest Lodging & Special Occasion Destination!"

WHAT TIME DO YOU WAKE UP EACH MORNING AND WHAT DOES YOUR **schedule look like?**

I wake up pretty normal hours, between 6 and 7am. We have an Innkeeper who is here to make breakfast and greet guests in the morning.

What is the most rewarding part of the job?

Seeing happy customers and hearing from brides and grooms who made amazing memories.

Do you need to be a great cook to run a B&B?

No, but it helps! You need to be able to cook with all your heart.

Can one person run a B&B themselves? At what point do you need help?

I think that any B & B with more than 4 rooms requires a staff.

How do you deal with check-ins and check-outs?

We try to greet all our guests, but for those arriving late we leave keys in a safe location for them to retrieve on their own. We see most guests out and wish them a wonderful journey.

TEN

Villa Cathedral

1202 Williamson Road
Alton, VA 24520

Lucy & Bill

WHAT TIME DO YOU WAKE UP EACH MORNING AND WHAT DOES YOUR schedule look like?

There is no schedule. When we have guests we are typically serving breakfast @ 6:30 and subsequently they are out the door for the day.

What is the most rewarding part of the job?

We meet interesting people from all over the country. Have only had a couple guests that we really didn't care for.

Do you need to be a great cook to run a B&B?

It helps. It seems most people don't cook much if at all and really enjoy a proper breakfast.

Can one person run a B&B themselves? At what point do you need help?

Not likely but if the bookings are sporadic I suppose it could be done by one workaholic. My wife and I have some PT help (when needed) for general cleaning and room prep.

How do you deal with check-ins and check-outs?

Vague question. We query people the day of check-in for an arrival time which is not accurate more times than it is. All our financials are handled via our booking engine that is linked to our website and channel managers to the OTAs.

ELEVEN

The Inn at Ragged Edge

1090 Ragged Edge Road
Chambersburg, PA 17202

Ken and Barb Kipe

WHAT TIME DO YOU WAKE UP EACH MORNING AND WHAT DOES YOUR schedule look like?

I wake up at 4:00am, work a full time job away from the Inn and then come home around 3:00pm and work at the Inn. Weekends full time at the Inn hosting weddings and events. My wife takes care of breakfasts, reservations and much of the cleaning.

What is the most rewarding part of the job?

Interacting with guests and hosting world renown pianists performing classical piano concerts.

Do you need to be a great cook to run a B&B?

A good breakfast is vital. My wife is an awesome cook.

Can one person run a B&B themselves? At what point do you need help?

One person can - depending on how many rooms they have. We have 9 guest rooms and host 25 weddings a year. We do 90% of everything ourselves.

How do you deal with check-ins and check-outs?

Personally greet and check in each guest. They can check out themselves if we are not around.

TWELVE

BlissWood Bed and Breakfast Ranch

13597 Frantz Road
Cat Spring, TX 78933

Carol Davis

- **2020 Tripadvisor Travelers' Choice Award**

- **2018 Certificate of Excellence – Hall of Fame Award Winner in TripAdvisor**

- **Host of The Bachelor – German Edition**

- **Southern Living 2016 – Top Historic Destination**

WHAT TIME DO YOU WAKE UP EACH MORNING AND WHAT DOES YOUR **schedule look like?**

5:30-6:00. No idea how my "Schedule looks like!" Could be different every day. Answering phone calls, e-mails, texts, scheduling staff, etc.

What is the most rewarding part of the job?

The joy I bring to people that come here.

Do you need to be a great cook to run a B&B?

Not necessarily

Can one person run a B&B themselves?

Well, I'm doing that! With housekeepers, ranch help.

At what point do you need help?

When you can't handle it yourself after working 7 days a week!

How do you deal with check-ins and check-outs?

Self-check-in, no check-in area, go direct to house/cabin. Check-outs, guests leave the keys and drive home! I have a schedule for staff listing all check-ins/check-outs.

THIRTEEN

Connellsville Bed and Breakfast

316 W. Crawford Avenue
Connellsville, PA 15425

Lucille King

**WHAT TIME DO YOU WAKE UP EACH MORNING AND WHAT DOES YOUR
schedule look like?**

I wake up at 5 a.m., make and serve breakfast; then see guests
off; clean rooms and do laundry. Maybe have a chance to relax a
little before welcoming guests and getting them settled.

What is the most rewarding part of the job?

The guests are interesting.

Do you need to be a great cook to run a B&B?

No, just be aware of food dislikes and allergies.

Can one person run a B&B themselves?

Only if one has less than 3 rooms. At what point do you need help? When one has 4 rooms or more, during high season.

How do you deal with check-ins and check-outs?

Guest ring the intercom. We answer the door to welcome them and guide them to their room. Go over all procedures and breakfast; answer any questions. Check-outs: Payment is done upon arrival. Usually, their credit card secures the reservation. After breakfast we walk them to the door or to the garage where their bicycles are stored. Say good-bye and wish them a good trip. We also help with any bicycle problems.

FOURTEEN

Hocking Hills Inn

13984 OH-664 Scenic
Logan, OH 43138

Linda Thomas

WHAT TIME DO YOU WAKE UP EACH MORNING AND WHAT DOES YOUR schedule look like?

5:30 am. Get ready and head to the Coffee Emporium (Next door to the Inn)

What is the most rewarding part of the job?

Guest satisfaction!

Do you need to be a great cook to run a B&B?

No, we offer signature breakfast panini, large voluptuous muffins & fresh brewed coffee

Can one person run a B&B themselves?

Not recommended

At what point do you need help?

There is always work to do, maintenance and prep.

How do you deal with check-ins and check-outs?

We send an email with detailed instructions. Our Inn suites each have their own coded door lock that is changed with every guest.

FIFTEEN

Miller Tree Inn

654 E Division St,
Forks, WA 98331

Susan Brager

**WHAT TIME DO YOU WAKE UP EACH MORNING AND WHAT DOES YOUR
schedule look like?**

Prior to Covid we were up at 6am unless we were feeding
fishermen earlier. I would be in bed by 9PM. My husband
stayed up later.

What is the most rewarding part of the job?

Satisfied guests and happy employees.

Do you need to be a great cook to run a B&B?

Most people are very grateful that someone is cooking for them.
I consider myself a good cook with an eye for presentation. I
don't consider myself to be a great cook.

**Can one person run a B&B themselves? At what point do you need
help?**

Maybe a one or two room inn can be run by one person. I
wouldn't do it, however.

How do you deal with check-ins and check-outs?

Things have changed since Covid. We have very limited contact
with people. They call us when they arrive. We show them their
room and then we typically don't see them again. We are doing
an "in room, to go" breakfast that we put in each room before the
guests arrive.

SIXTEEN

Ringling House Bed & Breakfast

201 8th Street
Baraboo, WI 53913

Julie Hearley & Stuart Koehler

WHAT TIME DO YOU WAKE UP EACH MORNING AND WHAT DOES YOUR
schedule look like?

- 6am- 9am Get up & set table & make & serve breakfast

- 9-10:30am clean up after breakfast

- 10:30-11am check people out & get payment

- 11am-1pm get cleaners started on rooms, bring up laundry & stock linens

- 1pm-3pm run errands, go shopping, take a nap

- 3pm-7pm check people in/offer wine & cheese

- 7pm-9pm have supper, do laundry,, put away clean dishes, watch TV, run errands

- 9pm-10:30pm - prep for breakfast

- 10:30pm-11:30pm - go to bed

- 7 days a week

What is the most rewarding part of the job?

- When we convert people from staying at a hotel to a B&B on a regular basis!

- Teaching people the history of Baraboo and the Ringling Family. We are keeping the rich history of the area alive with stories!

Do you need to be a great cook to run a B&B?

- I think it helps, but you don't need to be a chef. People love the homemade meals with quality ingredients they find here. I've heard of B&B's having continental breakfasts, and most B&B people we have talked to are not thrilled with this idea.

Can one person run a B&B themselves? At what point do you need help?

- It depends on the person, and the number of rooms they are renting out. If I only had two rooms, I think I could do it myself. We have six, are full every day in the summer, and there is no way I could keep up.

How do you deal with check-ins and check-outs?

- We have set times for check-in (4pm-7pm), which is different from the hotel industry, and can be confusing for those that have not been to a B&B before. We like to be here to personally check people in, but sometimes that does not work if someone needs to check in late. For these circumstances, we have a lockbox on the back door, where we can leave a guest a key to their room for self check in.

SEVENTEEN

Wayne Bed & Breakfast Inn

211 Strafford Avenue
Wayne, PA 19087

Traudi and Bob Thomason
Innkeepers

We were awarded the 2016 Small Business of the Year by the Main Line Chamber of Commerce.

WHAT TIME DO YOU WAKE UP EACH MORNING AND WHAT DOES YOUR schedule look like?

6:00AM and start preparing for Breakfast. After Breakfast, cleaning and organizing.

What is the most rewarding part of the job?

Guests and their 'stories'. We have had guests from 39 States and 38 Countries.

Do you need to be a great cook to run a B&B?

You become one.

Can one person run a B&B themselves?

Yes

At what point do you need help?

When occupancy exceeds 50%.

How do you deal with check-ins and check-outs?

With a good Booking System.

EIGHTEEN

Meadows Inn Bed & Breakfast

12013 US-20,
Middlebury, IN 46540

**WHAT TIME DO YOU WAKE UP EACH MORNING AND WHAT DOES YOUR
schedule look like?**

Every day is different. That is one of the best parts of being an
Innkeeper. Never a dull moment!

What is the most rewarding part of the job?

The Guests!

Do you need to be a great cook to run a B&B?

No, you don't need to be a great cook to run a B&B. You do need to be able to provide your guests with an exceptional breakfast.

Can one person run a B&B themselves? At what point do you need help?

This would depend on the size of the B&B. However, overall, it would be hard to run all aspects of a B&B on your own. The Innkeeper must be able to keep their focus on the guest experience.

How do you deal with check-ins and check-outs?

We provide our guests with flexible check- in times. Depending on the time of year, check-out can also be flexible. I always greet each guest personally upon arrival and say goodbye before they leave.

NINETEEN

The Lincoln Inn & Restaurant At The Covered Bridge

2709 W. Woodstock Road
Woodstock, Vermont 05091

Mara Mehlman
Proprietor

WHAT TIME DO YOU WAKE UP EACH MORNING AND WHAT DOES YOUR schedule look like?

Up at 6:00 am. In the kitchen by 7:00 am. My partner and chef starts breakfast prep.

What is the most rewarding part of the job?

Happy Guests.

Do you need to be a great cook to run a B&B?

Not to run a B&B. Just good hardy breakfast is enough. Having a good chef is important if you open a restaurant as part of the b&b.

Can one person run a B&B themselves? At what point do you need help?

No. We have a small team. We have two front of house staff and a housekeeper.

How do you deal with check-ins and check-outs?

In our case, it is more challenging because we also have a restaurant. We are busy throughout the day and evening. Check-in begins at 3:00 pm until 9:00 pm and check-out is by 11:00 am. We don't allow for late check-outs. We need to be able to get the housekeeper in to clean and turn the rooms.

TWENTY

Devonfield Inn

1800 Devonfield Inn
85 Stockbridge Road Lee, MA 01238

Doug & Jim
Innkeepers

-" Where to Stay in the Berkshires"- The New York Times

- 2020 Traveler's Choice by TripAdvisor

- 2020 Loved by Guests Award by Hotels.com

- 2020 Traveler's Review Award by Booking.com

- 2020 Best of Lee

- 2020 Top Ten Romantic Inns by iLoveInns.com

- 2020 Top Ten Accommodations in the Berkshires by
TravelMyth

WHAT TIME DO YOU WAKE UP EACH MORNING AND WHAT DOES YOUR schedule look like?

The day generally starts at 6am. Get to the inn and get the coffee on for those early rising guests. Then it's time to start to prep for breakfast. From 6 to about 8 the cooking and baking go on to be ready for our first guests at 8:15. From then till about 10am it is all about breakfast service. Getting the orders and keeping ahead of the crowds. When breakfast is through, it's all about clearing, cleaning and calculating what needs to be done next: get the housekeepers going as guests check out at 11am. Cleaning goes on till about 3pm when the next set of guests arrive. During that time usually 3 times a week its hitting all the food stores to stock up on groceries. Once three o'clock comes Doug will engage in paperwork and bill paying while I start the baking process for the next morning. From 3 till ideally 7pm we wait for the arrival of our guests to welcome them and give them the history and tour of the property. Hopefully by 7:30 we are sitting down to dinner. By 9pm it's watching TV in bed till we fall asleep, awaiting for the alarm to go off and it's time to start all over again.
Sometimes it feels like Groundhog's Day, the movie!

What is the most rewarding part of the job?

The most rewarding part of the job is all the wonderful people that you meet along the way. Guests arrive at the Inn as strangers but leave shortly thereafter as friends.

Do you need to be a great cook to run a B&B?

Food service all depends on what you choose to offer. We go from simple cheesy scrambled eggs to Veggie Quiches to Eggs Benedict to Breakfast Lasagna (and a ton of things in between). We find in addition to the cold buffet that offering guest the choice between a sweet and savory option is very well received. We also engage the services of "Guest Chefs" that work at local restaurants which helps ensure diversity in the daily menu.

Can one person run a B&B themselves? At what point do you need help?

Staffing is truly dependent on the size of your inn. Smaller Inns with 4-5 rooms are less likely to generate enough revenue to hire a staff so it would all fall on the shoulders of the innkeeper(s). Also seasonality plays a major variable. For us our high season is June - October and then it starts to quiet down a bit through the holidays into Feb. By March it is our quietest season so we employ staff members in accordance with the season.

How do you deal with check-ins and check-outs?

We pride ourselves on personal service so we do try to stay at the inn until every guest has arrived. Upon their arrival we greet them and offer them a tour of the house along with outlining some of the issues that they need to be aware of: where to park, how and when we serve breakfast. Also the house was built in 1800 with a very interesting history that we impart of the guests. We also like to be available to answer questions on best restaurants, activities in the area and places of interest. For check-outs it's the same - we like to personally say goodbye to each guest and talk with them to ascertain what type of guest experience they had and if their stay matched their expectations. Many B&B guests want interaction with the owners and doing so seems to have a big impact on their overall experience. Many will ask how we and why we got started in the business. Our story seems boring to us, but they often find it fascinating to hear.

TWENTY-ONE

Trillium Bed & Breakfast

5151 River Road, Niagara Falls,
Ontario L2E 3G8 Canada

Brian & Mary

**WHAT TIME DO YOU WAKE UP EACH MORNING AND WHAT DOES YOUR
schedule look like?**

I am usually up by 6:30am and quite busy until noon, then have
an hour or two before next guests check-in, sometimes waiting
until late at night for them to come.

Do you need to be a great cook to run a B&B?

You don't need to be a great cook, but a good one
would work well.

**Can one person run a B&B themselves? At what point do you need
help?**

I do run it by myself, with 3 rooms, any more
rooms and you would need someone to help.

TWENTY-TWO

Whistling Swan Inn

110 Main St.
Stanhope, NJ 07874

Rosalind Bruno
Owner/Innkeeper

**WHAT TIME DO YOU WAKE UP EACH MORNING AND WHAT DOES YOUR
schedule look like?**

I usually wake up at 6:00 a.m. The coffee is made first, because
without it, I'm not much good. Breakfast preparation must be
complete by 8:30. After breakfast is over and the kitchen cleaned
up, I usually go into my office to catch up on emails, etc. The
schedule for the remainder of the day varies depending upon
what needs to be done. I'll prep breakfast for the next day; bake
cookies or put together room enhancement packages. Of course,

these activities are customarily interrupted by phone calls or guest requests. Every day I do try to carve out at least 1 hour to rest, read, catch up with friends or indulge in what I like to call my beautification treatments. It's essential to long-term well-being.

What is the most rewarding part of the job?

The most rewarding part of the job is meeting new people. I love chatting with my guests – they're from all walks of life and doing interesting things.

Do you need to be a great cook to run a B&B?

Not really. My mother used to say "If you can read, you can cook", and to a certain extent it's true. I like trying new recipes, but have found that my guests go for simple and tasty, but not necessarily gourmet. We try to accommodate dietary restrictions, such as gluten free or vegan whenever possible and with appropriate advance notice.

Can one person run a B&B themselves? At what point do you need help?

I guess if someone has a small inn (fewer than 5 rooms), it's possible to run a B&B alone. Some of my colleagues certainly do, but I think doing everything yourself will contribute to burnout.

TWENTY-THREE

The Inn At Five Points

102 Lincoln Ave
Saratoga Springs, NY 12866

Eilis & Jim Petrosino

Tripadvisor Certificate of Excellence 2016-2020 (Every year we've been open)

WHAT TIME DO YOU WAKE UP EACH MORNING AND WHAT DOES YOUR schedule look like?

Get house in condition for guests (clean up overnight glassware, garbage, pick up, put furniture or pillows back, wash glasses and put back out), Set up for breakfast services, run coffee, heat hot water, prep breakfast, serve breakfast, clean up from breakfast, sit down for calls, emails and correspondence, guest check ins, concierge services, grocery shopping on most days, another round of calls, emails and correspondence, happy hour to mingle with guests, dinner privately, odds and ends, cleaning living areas again and checking rooms while guests are out to dinner that housekeeping has done a good enough job, restock coffee cart and put out sign that we've turned in.

What is the most rewarding part of the job?

When a guest writes a review and reminds us why we do it all.

Do you need to be a great cook to run a B&B?

No, you need to know how to do a few things well!

Can one person run a B&B themselves? At what point do you need help?

I would say it depends on how big it is BUT it would be a full time around the clock job if they did. I would think anyone would still need help with things like; Housekeeping, website updates and design, possible marketing and upkeep of the home (a handy man, plumber, etc).

How do you deal with check-ins and check-outs?

We check all guests in personally unless they are checking in outside of the 3-7pm check in time then we email them information or text (or both) and do a self check in. The more you can help and show guests what is on property at time of check in the less questions and information you'll have to provide while they are there.. We find most guests get annoyed if they find they cannot get something quickly because they don't know how + cant always get in touch with us right away. People want instant gratification + without sitting in the main dining area 24/7 you'll need to make sure they have all the information they can have. We have signs, emails, on our website info, maps of area, our favorites brochures, a welcome book, etc.

TWENTY-FOUR

Hummingbird Inn

14 N Aurora Street
Easton, MD 21601

Eric
Owner

- 2018, 2020 Chesapeake Readers Choice Award "Best Bed & Breakfast"

- 2020 Chesapeake Readers Choice Award "Best Breakfast"

- 2020 Chesapeake Readers Choice Runner-Up for "Best Hotel"

- 2018, 2019, 2020 Trip Advisors "Award of Excellence"

- 2017, 2018, 2019, 2020 Booking.com "Travel Review Award"

- 2018, 2019 Yelp "People Love Us Award"

- Some of our other achievements include being the location shoot for a soon-to-be-release feature film on Amazon Prime called "The Detour" about a guy that inherits a B&B in a small town. We also have been selected to be a "Dream Vacation Giveaway" on the national TV game show, "The Price Is Right" (air-date TBD).

WHAT TIME DO YOU WAKE UP EACH MORNING AND WHAT DOES YOUR schedule look like?

It depends on the number of guests staying that night. With 75% or more full, I'm usually up around 5am to get started (getting coffee station going, start prepping what needs to be prepped if it wasn't done the night before, etc.). Breakfast service is from 8:30 – 10:00. Because of COVID, if we have more than 4 rooms booked, then we do 2 separate scheduled seating's vs. our regular open seating. That way we can make sure that everyone has their own table and the tables are appropriately spaced apart. When we do 2 seating, we do 8:00am – 9:00am for seating #1, then 30 min to reset and 2nd seating is from 9:30am – 10:30am. After breakfast, checkout is 11:00am and then cleanup. During non-COVID times, we then will refresh any room that is going to be occupied the next night by the same guest (make the bed, replace bathroom amenities, etc.). We aren't doing that now as we don't go into rooms once a guest checks in. If a guest is checking out, then housekeeping will go in and do a full reset/clean of the room. After that we start prepping for checking which is 3pm – 5pm but occasionally there are guests requesting to check-in early which we try to always accommodate if we can. Next is check-in and following that we begin prepping for breakfast the next morning. In the evenings, we can be involved with either dog-sitting (we are a dog friendly B&B and also offer our guests on-site sitting service if guests are going out to dinner and cannot take their pup), we also offer our guests "Porch Time" where we will bring out snacks, some wine, and hangout on the porch with the guests listening to music, socializing, etc. We try to shut everything down by 10pm so we can get some rest and then start the fun all over again the next morning. And when I say "fun", I'm being sincere – it IS fun. It's work, and there's a lot to do, but if you're doing what you love it really is fun.

What is the most rewarding part of the job?

Meeting great people, making new friends, knowing that guests are thoroughly enjoying their stay, and seeing guests return again and again.

Do you need to be a great cook to run a B&B?

Someone does. People come to B&B's not just to sleep, but to have the full experience. In my opinion, that includes the breakfast. Otherwise it'd just be a motel/hotel. I know there are many different interpretations on what constitutes "breakfast" at different B&B's, but my vision included a full, 3-course gourmet breakfast complete with home baked goods, unique/international menu options, and breakfast cocktails.

Can one person run a B&B themselves? At what point do you need help?

Yes – I did when I first opened. But that was when business was slow and just getting going. Once more rooms are getting booked you would want help with a top-notch housekeeping team and it then goes on from there. Of course it also depends on what size B&B you have. If it just has a couple of rooms, it's conceivable that one person could run it alone all the time. However, I think if you have 3 or 4 (or more) rooms, you will want help. As I stated before, I love this life, but we all need a break so you don't burn-out too soon. Even getting off the property during the day, in the evenings, etc. is very important.

How do you deal with check-ins and check-outs?

There's always someone from the Inn Staff at the Inn to do both check-in and check-out. For check-in, guests are greeted, they fill out/sign the registration form, then they are presented with the breakfast menu for the next day. We offer our guests a choice of 2 entrees and 3 side dishes. We have our guests place their orders the night before so we know exactly what we need to prep and don't end up with food waste. Once they complete that, we take them on a short tour of the common areas and then we assist them up to their rooms. Once in the room, they get a few more information about the Inn, the room, access in/out during their stay, answer any questions, then leave them from there. For check-out, once guests are ready to leave, they come down to the from lobby and return their keys and any open balances are settled. We then print out their reservation folio and set them on their way.

TWENTY-FIVE

Tinder Guest House

106 S Railroad Ave
Ashland, Virginia 23005

Sharon McKenna

**WHAT TIME DO YOU WAKE UP EACH MORNING AND WHAT DOES YOUR
schedule look like?**

Wow! Prior to my redesign due to C-19, I got up by at least 7
am to cook the breakfast casserole. I had someone else clean
every day. Now, I check folks in after 3pm or later, and I'm done
until they check-out, unless they are staying more than 3 days, if
so, I replenish the breakfast treats and take out the trash- it's
easy!

What is the most rewarding part of the job?

The most rewarding part of the job is my reviews which show how much the guests enjoyed themselves. They have also left me presents an antique lamp, a Christmas painting of Santa on a train, Christmas stockings, for example.

Do you need to be a great cook to run a B&B?

Be a great cook- not me! But I have some really great recipes and tricks of the trade friends have taught me.

Can one person run a B&B themselves? At what point do you need help?

I pretty much run it myself now, but help is really important. If my husband weren't my handyman, I would have to hire someone. And, if I am sick, someone else has to do what I do.

How do you deal with check-ins and check-outs?

I personally check folks in, there is no check-out process. All fees are paid two weeks before check-in. If the booking is in less than two weeks, full payment must be made prior to check-in.

TWENTY-SIX

Weller Haus Bed Breakfast & Event Center

319 Poplar St
Bellevue, Kentucky 41073

WHAT TIME DO YOU WAKE UP EACH MORNING AND WHAT DOES YOUR schedule look like?

AS LATE AS POSSIBLE! Seriously, depends on how many rooms we have booked the night before. We have 5 rooms and if we're full, 6:30 am for breakfast ramp up. The day depends on what else is going on. We also have an Event Venue as part of our property and we do weddings. During wedding season, it's usually getting set up for a wedding if it's a weekend. Other times (spring-fall) it's tending to our gardens which are expansive. Answering emails. Responding to phone calls. Giving tours of the event venue and meeting with customers about booking weddings and/or other events. We have a housekeeping staff of 3-4 part-timers so all of the room cleaning is left to that group.

What is the most rewarding part of the job?

For me, it's the flexible lifestyle….not a routine 9-5 situation.

Do you need to be a great cook to run a B&B?

I think a good deal of the customers that select a B&B are "food people" and expect a good breakfast…..so I think you need to know what you're doing in the kitchen.

Can one person run a B&B themselves? At what point do you need help?

In my case, no. But it depends on the size of your business. If you have a one-room B&B that you're renting out for some extra cash….sure. But you have to decide what's more important—ponying up some payroll so you can have staff do the cleaning and you can take care of things that matter—marketing, website updating, etc., etc,, or if you want to have your head stuck in the cleaning bucket from the moment you finish breakfast. We do not require a two-night minimum on the weekends so there are times my staff is turning over five rooms in four hours…..if I had made that choice to do the cleaning myself---I would not have lasted the 17 years that I've been here. I didn't get into this business to clean. You have to remember why you chose to do it and I'm guessing you won't run across one innkeeper/owner that says "so I could clean rooms every day". You will know when you need additional help…depends on your business— occupancy and where you draw the line on where your time is more valuable.

How do you deal with check-ins and check-outs?

In the past, we greeted every guest between 3-6 pm and offered self check-in only for those guests that were planning to arrive after 6 pm. It got very tiresome very quickly waiting for people that gave us an estimated arrival time of say—4 pm…..and then showed up at 6. And never bothered to call. My time is valuable and I do have a personal life as well—so sitting and waiting for someone when I made dinner plans based on what they told me really started getting old. So first we started offering two types of check-ins---a "self check in" where they are not greeted by anyone. We provide them directions to their suite in an email along with their personal pin code for the room. Or they could opt for a "greeted" check in. If they made this choice, they needed to be on time. They were advised that if they gave me an arrival time of 4 pm and were not here by 4:15, it automatically switched to a self check in. With covid—we have gone completely to self check in and have no plans of offering a greeted check in any longer. Things come up for people and they run behind and we're not the priority for notification. First timers seem to think that we're like hotels with big old front desks and three reps there just waiting for them to stroll in at any time. This is probably one of the biggest pet peeves I have about this business....that and people that over indulge in the complimentary items we offer--People that fill their personal coolers with our complimentary soft drinks on their way out the door to go home

TWENTY-SEVEN

The Publishing House Bed and Breakfast

108 N May St
Chicago, Illinois 60607

Kimberly

**We've been featured in Dwell, 25 best hotels in Chicago
Conde Nast, Wallpaper, USA Today, Du Jour, CN Traveler,
Midwest living publications. Been featured on HGTV "You
Live in What?" and The Jam.**

WHAT TIME DO YOU WAKE UP EACH MORNING AND WHAT DOES YOUR
schedule look like?

I wake up at 6:30am to start breakfast by 7:30 or 8am (depending on the day) and finish around 5 or 6pm. The day transitions from breakfast, to cleaning, to checking guests in and administrative stuff.

What is the most rewarding part of the job?

Instant feedback. Many jobs you have to wait to see the final result, but you can engage with guests and change their experience in minutes. That is the reward to long hours and hard work.

Do you need to be a great cook to run a B&B?

You should always be passionate. You don't have to be Michelan star, but you should do what you do well. I love breakfast and like to add some creativity to the menu. Use good ingredients. People notice and it shows in the food.

Can one person run a B&B themselves? At what point do you need help?

I wouldn't know, I have an 11 room B&B and always need staff. However as an owner I am running it by myself.

How do you deal with check-ins and check-outs?

Ideally in person, but for afterhours we send instructions to our guests to checkin. Checkout we just ask them to leave the key in the door. There is no need to keep a person at a desk all day.

TWENTY-EIGHT

Westbrook Inn Bed and Breakfast

976 Boston Post Rd
Westbrook, CT 06498

Meri

- 5 star rating on Trip Advisor, Booking.com, Expedia.com, Google and other sites.

- We won the Best of the Shoreline in 2020 and the Trip Advisor travel award for 2020. I am on the Board of Directors for the CT Central Region Tourism board, and the Connecticut Lodging Association.

- I represented B&Bs on the Covid Re-open committee for the lodging.

WHAT TIME DO YOU WAKE UP EACH MORNING AND WHAT DOES YOUR schedule look like?

I've evolved over the past year to be more mindful about what guests really want. After some earlier starts, our breakfasts now start at 8 and guest have a 1 hour window to eat, with coffee available anytime. That allows me to get started around 6:30 – serve breakfast from 8-9, and then finish cleaning up breakfast by 10 or so. From there, check out good-byes are until 11am. Start with room cleaning and turnovers until about 2. We offer bikes and kayaks, so there may be time checking those items out. Some days I can sneak office work in before 3, and then check in's start. I usually can finish up next day prep, office work, wedding contracts, marketing calls, and work with a few B2B groups I'm involved with allowing me to leave about 6 or 7 pm. Luckily I have staff who do the room cleaning and laundry, though there are times I tackle it all myself. Then there is maintenance – my husband handles most of it, but since I am always on property, I do quite a bit too. What we can't do ourselves, we hire out.

The Pandemic was helpful in shifting guests to contactless check in, which is a big help. Before that I would sometimes have to wait for hours for guests who were scheduled to check in at 4 but didn't show up until 9 or later. Now we have locks which are custom to their phone number and provide all the information they need in their rooms. We continue to look for ways technology and innovation can help with labor costs and streamline operations, without impacting guest experience.

What is the most rewarding part of the job?

The guests – they are wonderful. We have met the best people and we feel so lucky to be part of these wonderful souls lives.

Do you need to be a great cook to run a B&B?

You need to be a creative cook and focus on what you do well. I am not a baker, but I found great local sources for scones and other delectables. People love that we support other local businesses and they also like they can visit those places and take a little piece of CT home with them.

Can one person run a B&B themselves? At what point do you need help?

It depends on size, and type of operation. If you are a lifestyle inn, then you are essentially inviting people into your home and looking to cover expenses. As a financially viable operation with any more than 5 rooms – doing it alone would be tricky. We have a 10 room Inn – I have done it myself in the slow times and while it's possible, something always will suffer. As an Innkeeper you need to be adept at customer relations, cooking, cleaning, decorating, laundry, website management, marketing, guest experience, revenue management, networking, SEO, booking, selling, plumbing, light maintenance, a local concierge, bookkeeping, banking and keeping up with local ordinances and that's just on a Monday!! It's very tough to tackle without staff or a big revenue stream to outsource activities.

How do you deal with check-ins and check-outs?

I spoke about check in's above. We used to great them personally and give them a tour of the property. Now we have shifted to contactless check in with a warm welcome note in the room, and in information letter. This also allows the guest to check in at their leisure and we honestly have not had any complaints on this practice. We will keep it, and we will do more to improve the welcome package in the rooms and introduce text communication to stay more closely connected with our guests. Check out we typically are there to thank the guest, invite them to sign the guest book and provide a warm send off. Breakfast is the key time when I get to interact with every guest, and I find it make the most impact.

TWENTY-NINE

The Bevin House Bed & Breakfast

26 Barton Hill Rd
East Hampton, CT 06424

Dean

WHAT TIME DO YOU WAKE UP EACH MORNING AND WHAT DOES YOUR schedule look like?

Wake up time is 7:00am to have breakfast ready for 8:30am .
Most prepared the night before makes it easy.

What is the most rewarding part of the job?

Meeting people from around the world & talking with them.
Also having them compliment you on the scrumptious breakfast
you just served.

Do you need to be a great cook to run a B&B?

Great? no, Good? yes. At least able to follow directions in a
cookbook if not. I like to be adventurous in my cooking. We
don't serve the plain & jane breakfasts. No scrambled eggs,
omelets, etc. Overnight orange/blueberry baked french toast
casserole with cheesy baked potatoes casserole

Can one person run a B&B themselves? At what point do you need help?

Absolutely, we only have 6 rooms but if you're organized it's not
a problem. Starting this year we are now hosting events, we'll
see if additional help is needed

How do you deal with check-ins and check-outs?

The hardest part about check-ins is waiting for the arrival, with no eta your constantly looking for the guests since you don't have a receptionist. Checking out consists of saying good-by and hope to see you again.

THIRTY

Secrets on Main Bed & Breakfast

314 S Main St
Cheboygan, Michigan 49721

Laurie Musclow

WHAT TIME DO YOU WAKE UP EACH MORNING, AND WHAT DOES YOUR schedule look like?

We start breakfast preparations the prior evening. The table is set after 11pm and if a breakfast casserole is on the menu, it is ready to bake in the morning. We are up at 7:30am and serve breakfast at 9am, unless other arrangements are requested.

Checkout is 11 and we begin stripping beds and laundry immediately after checkouts. We clean each room and have them ready for our next guests by 3 pm. Checkin is 4, but some arrive early. The afternoon is spent cleaning and baking cookies that are available all evening in the Beverage Center. Muffins are available at 7am. Evenings we are available to our guests and we offer marshmallows around the fire pit and visit and monitor the fire until the last guest heads to their room.

What is the most rewarding part of the job?

When guests return again and again! And knowing that we offered them a memory that they will talk about for years to come.

Do you need to be a great cook to run a B&B?

Absolutely not! BUT - one should like baking and being in the kitchen! Recipes are plentiful and great resources. Having a few recipes for glutton and lactose intolerant guests is necessary as well. We try to use fresh local ingredients when we can and tell our guests that information.

Can one person run a B&B by themselves? At what point do you need help?

We work as a team. We both put breakfast together. Outside maintenance is constant, as is keeping the inside spotless. Baking is ongoing as well. It would not be impossible to run a B&B solo, but the owner could face potential burnout quickly. This summer we are hiring someone to clean the rooms, hopefully freeing our time to include relaxation.

How do you deal with checkins and checkouts?

Checkin is set from 4 to 7 pm. Often though guests are driving a distance and arrive later. Most call us so we are aware, but occasionally guests arrive after 10 pm. We just roll with it! Checkout is at 11 - and sometimes we are asked for a late checkout, which we can extend to noon, but with guests coming in right behind the departing guests, it can be difficult.

THIRTY-ONE

Harvest Barn Inn

16 Webb Terrace #3157
Bellows Falls, VT 05101

Rich & Ellen

WHAT TIME DO YOU WAKE UP EACH MORNING AND WHAT DOES YOUR
schedule look like?

A typical day would be 7am or a bit earlier, coffee on, breakfast
served 8:30am (during COVID we staggered breakfast times),
breakfast clean-up around 9:30am, guests leave 11am. We
change beddings/vacuum/clean bathrooms and restock supplies.
Check in time is 3pm but we must be ready earlier as some
guests will show up when they want.

What is the most rewarding part of the job?

Independence - if you are organized it is nice passive income
with plenty of free time. You meet great people and live in a nice
house with great views.

Do you need to be a great cook to run a B&B?

It is helpful to have some good baking skills. Ellen has taken that
role and has gotten many compliments on her cookies and
scones.

Can one person run a B&B themselves?

It can be done, but I don't think it would be enjoyable. Ellen and
I have split up some tasks based on our likes and strengths, she
handles all the bookkeeping, baking, laundry and most breakfast
dishes and bed making. We share room turn-overs, I am the
bathroom cleaner, stripping the bedding and restocking.

At what point do you need help?

One year I (Rich) was working outside the Inn part-time, we
needed help in the busy season and got someone who would help
flip a room about 4 hours a week.

How do you deal with check-ins and check-outs?

Check in is 3pm-7pm, although some people have shown up as early as 11:30am and as late as 2am! Depending on the circumstances, we sometimes take in early check-ins or ask them to come back later. Usually the very late arrivals are missed or delayed flights, they are very grateful that we stayed up to greet them. The check in process in an introduction to our services- coffee/tea station and to show them their rooms. Also, we will make dinner recommendations if they like.

THIRTY-TWO

The Grand Kerr House

17777 Beaver St
Grand Rapids, OH 43522

~

Bob & Cathy Trame

WHAT TIME DO YOU WAKE UP EACH MORNING AND WHAT DOES YOUR schedule look like?

With guests at the house, we are up by 7:00 to prepare and serve breakfast (served between 8:00 and 10:00). Then breakfast clean up (no dishwasher as we serve on china), guest check out by noon then we clean the rooms and start laundry (need have two sets of linens for every room), new guest check in between 4:00 and 6:00, house tour and getting guest settled in can take one to two hours. Normally in bed by 10:00. Additionally, Cathy works outside the home and is responsible for reservations, paying bills and related paperwork. Bob is in charge of house maintenance and yard work. Cathy does the baking and Bob makes breakfast.

What is the most rewarding part of the job?

Sharing our home and it's history with guests who really appreciate Victorian homes. It's rare to have a guest that we do not find some common ground with.

Do you need to be a great cook to run a B&B?

It's good to have a signature breakfast recipe (or two). Bob has a great reputation for his omelettes made to order (people will call and ask if they can just come to breakfast without staying overnight) and Cathy always has fresh chocolate chip cookies in the room and pumpkin bread on the table. For guests staying more than one night we will usually ask them what their favorite breakfast is and serve that. Every breakfast includes bacon, fresh fruit, juice, coffee and tea. People so rarely sit down and enjoy breakfast that they are thrilled to find a nicely set table and a hot meal.

Can one person run a B&B themselves? At what point do you need help?

For a B&B with four rooms or less, one person might be able to manage the quick cleaning of the guests rooms, laundry, housework and doing the paperwork. But, like any home, if there is only one of you, you may need to hire out the maintenance and yard work. If there is only one of you, I would suggest starting out with only two rooms and then increasing bed count as you develop your routines. Better to have a few happy guests than a single disgruntled one.

How do you deal with check-ins and check-outs?

We have a two hour window for check-in (4:00 to 6:00) with check-out by noon. One of us is always on-site for check-in and check-out. At check-in we complete paperwork and collect payment if due. The house orientation and tour can take ten minutes to an hour, depending on the guest. We have a small bell on the dining room table for guests to ring when checking out, just to make sure we get to thank them for coming and get so say good-bye.

THIRTY-THREE

The Bear's Den B&B

864 Driftwood
Page, Arizona 86040

Bubba & Deb-b Ketchersid

WHAT TIME DO YOU WAKE UP EACH MORNING AND WHAT DOES YOUR schedule look like?

In season, April – Oct, my day starts at 5:00 am to get breakfast ready for my guests. After they depart or head out for the day I start my cleaning. Check-in's start around 3:00 pm and on a good day I am done around 11:00 pm.

What is the most rewarding part of the job?

People! When you can take care of someone's needs or wants it is a great reward. When they check out and tell you this has been the best experience they have had in a B&B it really makes it worth it.

Do you need to be a great cook to run a B&B?

No, but you learn fast. My first guests were not as fortunate as my guests are today.

Can one person run a B&B themselves? At what point do you need help?

I pretty much run by B&B by myself as my wife works full time. We only have 3 rooms so it is manageable. We do not bring anyone in when we take time off, we want to keep our rep at the highest levels.

How do you deal with check-ins and check-outs?

I meet and greet each and every guest. I show them personally their room and explain the amenities and where everything is located. It means a lot to each guest and reduces the questions or challenges in the long run.

THIRTY-FOUR

The Oaks Bed and Breakfast

516 Oak Avenue
Sulphur Springs, TX 75482

Allison Libby-Thesing

WHAT TIME DO YOU WAKE UP EACH MORNING AND WHAT DOES YOUR schedule look like?

My alarm goes off right now at 7, corona changed that for me. Before it was 6 so I could get my kids off to school. My schedule is simple when it come to the B& B; cook breakfast, serve, visit with guests, clean up the kitchen. Once guests check out clean rooms. Make sure everything is ready for the next guest.

What is the most rewarding part of the job?

I really enjoy meeting all our guests and getting to know them. We visit with everyone and try to find out about their lives.

Do you need to be a great cook to run a B&B?

Probably not a great cook but you should have some skills with breakfast.

Can one person run a B&B themselves? At what point do you need help?

For the most part yes, one person can do it all, depending on how many rooms. We only have three rooms which is very manageable for one person. If we had more rooms or an event the same day as guests checking in and out then help would be handy.

How do you deal with check-ins and check-outs?

We try to make it as easy as possible for our guests. We send check in instructions the day before arrival and we usually discuss check out at breakfast.

THIRTY-FIVE

Isabella B&B

1009 Church Street
Port Gibson, MS 39150

Bobbye Pinnix

**WHAT TIME DO YOU WAKE UP EACH MORNING AND WHAT DOES YOUR
schedule look like?**

My day starts at 5:00 AM and ends about 10:00 PM. Depending
on the needs of guests I serve breakfast from 7:00 to 8:30, clean
the kitchen and start to clean rooms as soon as guests leave so
that I will be prepared for the 3:00 PM check-in.

What is the most rewarding part of the job?

Meeting people from all over the world and all walks of life.

Do you need to be a great cook to run a B&B?

No but it helps. Some innkeepers are fortunate enough to hire someone to come in to prepare breakfast.

Can one person run a B&B themselves? At what point do you need help?

One person can if they are middle age with lots of energy. It really depends on how many rooms you have. One or two rooms can easily be managed by one person but anything over that becomes difficult.

How do you deal with check-ins and check-outs?

I am always at home and available for both. My B&B is operated out of the home that I live in.

THIRTY-SIX

Sage Hill Inn & Spa

4444 Ranch to Market Rd 150
Kyle, Texas 78640

Brad Burkhart
General Manager

We have the certificate of excellence from trip advisor for the past 4 years running. We also have recognition of excellence from hotels combined.

WHAT TIME DO YOU WAKE UP EACH MORNING AND WHAT DOES YOUR schedule look like?

I start the day at 8 AM every morning. I have start that starts as early as 6:30 am for the restaurant. I will stay until around 5 or 6. I have staff here until 8 or 10 depending on the weekday/weekend.

What is the most rewarding part of the job?

Speaking with our guests is the most rewarding part of the job. I love seeing and talking with a happy guest.

Do you need to be a great cook to run a B&B?

You don't need to be a great cook but it sure does help. I hire a chef to provide yummy food.

Can one person run a B&B themselves? At what point do you need help?

I could not imagine one person running b&b unless you only had a few rooms. We have 20 rooms/cottages/casitas total. I have 20 staff members.

How do you deal with check-ins and check-outs?

With covid we are doing everything remotely. We call each and everyone of our guest for check-in and check-outs. Before covid I would give each guest a private tour upon arrival.

THIRTY-SEVEN

The Dolon House

5 W Broadway
Jim Thorpe, PA 18229

Michael Rivkin

**WHAT TIME DO YOU WAKE UP EACH MORNING AND WHAT DOES YOUR
schedule look like?**

We rise about 6:30 and are down in the kitchen by 7:30 for 9:00 breakfast service [we live on site]. Breakfast usually goes til 10 or 10:30. Check-out is at 11, and then time to clean rooms and the Inn for arriving guests. Check-in from 3 to 7. Dinner break for us. Set and prep for breakfast. Retire about 11.

What is the most rewarding part of the job?

We really love the guest interaction, and have become good friends with many, many of them!! Some come 5 or 6 times a year!

Do you need to be a great cook to run a B&B?

No, but to be a good cook is useful. It really depends on the focus you give your breakfast. Here at The Dolon House, it is one of our top draws. I think in these times of AirBnB proliferation, a special breakfast is part of what sets a B&B apart, and can really help create one's signature.

Can one person run a B&B themselves? At what point do you need help?

No!!.... To properly be able to spend time assisting or just interacting with guests, and getting all the tasks done that are needed, requires two people to be able to balance and 'tag-team'.

How do you deal with check-ins and check-outs?

Interesting question. Despite very heavy emphasis on our 3PM starting check-in time, guests regularly arrive earlier. We simply need to politely remind them of the 3:00 arrival time, while we finish preparing the house for them [especially under Covid times]. Check-out is at 11; similarly we do need to remind folks of that too.

THIRTY-EIGHT

Historic Elgin Hotel

115 N Third
Marion, KS 66861

Tammy

**WHAT TIME DO YOU WAKE UP EACH MORNING AND WHAT DOES YOUR
schedule look like?**

I wake up at 6:45A to take my kids to school. Then I work out at the gym and come in to work about 9:30-10 and work till 5. During the day I do everything from answering phones, financials, marketing, laundry, attend meetings, etc.

What is the most rewarding part of the job?

Experiencing the joy and surprise when people arrive.

Do you need to be a great cook to run a B&B?

Not necessarily, although it helps. In the beginning, I did the cooking when we first opened. Then I trained staff to do the cooking. Now we prepare a made-from-scratch meal and put it in the room fridge for guests to heat at their convenience during the week. On Saturday and Sunday, we have our Kitchen Manager come in and prepare breakfast.

Can one person run a B&B themselves? At what point do you need help?

Depending on the size, yes, but I don't advise it. This would be a way to certainly burn yourself out! The point at which you need help is when you are working more hours than you want to be or are doing things that you hate to do. Life is too short to work too much or do work that you detest.

How do you deal with check-ins and check-outs?

Weekdays guests self check-in and out. Friday through Sunday, we have a guest services representative at our front desk that checks guests in and out. Bills are paid in full at check in.

THIRTY-NINE

Castle La Crosse Bed and Breakfast

1419 Cass St
La Crosse, WI 54601

Billy Bergeron & Brandon Rigger

WHAT TIME DO YOU WAKE UP EACH MORNING AND WHAT DOES YOUR **schedule look like?**

We wake up about 6:30 to have fresh coffee ready by 7:00. Breakfast is served daily at 9:00, either in private dining areas on the main floor or in the guest rooms. We had enjoyed a few years of serving breakfast in the dining room, buffet style for all the guests to chat and share stories, but that has changed with COVID-19. Dishes are cleared after everyone has finished, some linger and enjoy the seating areas on the main floor. Around the fire in cooler months or out on the front porch if the weather is nice. Check out time is 11:00, if it is time for the guests to leave there is a lot of moving around during that time. At times, some couples are leaving at the same time. They all need to be thanked and given a brochure to take, then check their rooms for anything left behind. Breakfast dishes may have to wait as rooms need to be made ready for more guests arriving at check in time, 3:00. It is only when breakfast has run later than normal because of good conversation that the next group of guests will want to check in early, narrowing your window of time to "flip" the room and clean the bathrooms. Lots of cleaning may be needed, spills cleaned up, taking out trash cans from the rooms, mopping and vacuuming, new linens on the bed. It's a long list, then double check to make sure all is in place. The afternoon is busy with guests arriving, telling the story of the house again, a tour of the main floor and dinner suggestions. Then we start to make breakfast for the following day if some things can be made ahead of time. We need to create a different breakfast daily, especially for guests staying several nights. This may involve running to the farmers market or grocery store. Back to that laundry you started when you stripped the beds at 11:00, then ironing pillow cases and cloth napkins for breakfast. In warmer weather, there is the lawn to mow or other projects that take up the afternoon. Guests check in between 3:00 - 6:00, then usually leave for dinner. While they are gone, we go into the suites to turn down the beds, close the blinds, check the towels and leave fresh baked cookies. This would also be time to check for trash that needs to be removed and turn on bedside lamps for their return. Guests typically return at a regular time after dinner, about 9:00, but at times it may be much later. The latest a couple has returned from a wedding was 4:30 a.m. It is only after all guests are in that we turn off the outside lights and lock up for the night. There are motion detectors to let us know if there is anyone moving around at night that may need something, most often a forgotten phone charger they left in the car, which means a run downstairs, unlock doors and turn on lights, then turn everything back off, lock up again and back to bed. Occasionally a guest will call during the night, which rings to my cell phone, to ask for more heat, less heat, more towels or the WiFi password.

Then....Repeat! There are days off to rest and enjoy, vacation times, too. You just have to mark those off on your calendar ahead of time.

What is the most rewarding part of the job?

Most rewarding are the stories from our guests and friendships we have made. The stories could fill a book and probably should! The friendships are very rewarding, we have gone to visit guests that have stayed with us and have made some good friends to travel with in the future. When we are not busy, we get to live in a grand home that is enjoying all the activity and attention.

Do you need to be a great cook to run a B&B?

It helps, I happen to be married to a wonderful chef. Chef Brandon graduated from Le Notre Culinary Institute just before we found the house for sale. He has control of his kitchen and enjoys creating a menu from the fresh ingredients we find in the area. That said, basic good and healthy food is acceptable too. We are known for our food, other B&B are known for their view from the deck in the back or their amazing massage therapist. Our guests want a very comfortable room and great food, other B&B guests want luxury and pampering, others want a spa and then there are those that want to be near the nightlife in a bustling downtown.

Can one person run a B&B themselves? At what point do you need help?

One person can run a B&B, we have heard of a couple of those. In those cases, much of the food is prepared beforehand, possibly by a local chef or restaurant. There are enough things to do to spit up equally between a couple, but if one person had to do it all, it's possible. I would think with a limited number of rooms it could be done. Once you get more than three rooms, some help would be wise. Even if that is a college student part-time that cleans the kitchen and baths or makes beds. Decide what is most time consuming and have them do that! Some B&B have a chef, most of those are more of an Inn that also serves dinner, so the chef is busy.

How do you deal with check-ins and check-outs?

Check-In and Check-Out at Castle La Crosse is very easy, we do not have a front desk, everything is done online when they make a reservation. Room keys are in the door of their rooms, once they arrive and get settled, they can take that key and lock up their room if they want. After check out, an automated email is sent thanking them for their stay, inviting them back and asking them to leave us an outstanding review with a link provided to do so. If we have guests, someone is always in the house in case the guests need something.

FORTY

Dragonfly Ranch

84-5146 Keala O Keawe Rd
Captain Cook, Hawaii 96704

Barbara Moore
Soul Proprietor

**WHAT TIME DO YOU WAKE UP EACH MORNING AND WHAT DOES YOUR
schedule look like?**

For decades, my schedule started at 6 AM and ended at
midnight. Now that I am 76 years old, I let other people get up
early and start breakfast and help me with all the email that I
need to attend to.

What is the most rewarding part of the job?

I love helping people with FlowerEssences, detoxifying cleanse and nutrition. I love helping people heal themselves.

Do you need to be a great cook to run a B&B?

I am very good at steaming vegetables. Some people find that simple food that is organic and nutritious is also delicious.

Can one person run a B&B themselves? At what point do you need help?

One person can wear themselves ragged trying to run a bed-and-breakfast alone.

How do you deal with check-ins and check-outs?

I have a team of people helping me.

FORTY-ONE

Ala Kai B&B

15 - 782 Paradise Ala Kai
Keaau, HI 96749

Erich Zipse & Suzy Chaffee

WHAT TIME DO YOU WAKE UP EACH MORNING AND WHAT DOES YOUR
schedule look like?

I'm up with the sun and sometimes before. I work almost every
day preparing the property, doing maintenance, setting up
accounts, getting the booking engines up and running on VRBO,
Expedia and Booking.com.

What is the most rewarding part of the job?

I love to see the place looking so good. We don't have any guests
yet.

Do you need to be a great cook to run a B&B?

Suzy and I are both great breakfast cooks. But, we are really
considering a breakfast basket either delivered to the dining area
on the outdoor lanai or the rooms.

**Can one person run a B&B themselves? At what point do you need
help?**

I think it would be difficult to run a B&B by myself. I have not
tried it yet.

FORTY-TWO

The Inn at Onancock

30 North St
Onancock, Virginia 23417

Kim
Owner/Innkeeper

- **Top 25 Bed and Breakfast in North America by BedandBreakfast.com in 2017.**

- **We have a 9.9 rating on Booking.com.**

- **We have received a 5-star Certificate of Excellence every year from TripAdvisor and were named to their top 10% of properties reviewed worldwide in 2020.**

- **We also were named Best Bed & Breakfast in the 2020 Locals Choice awards.**

WHAT TIME DO YOU WAKE UP EACH MORNING AND WHAT DOES YOUR schedule look like?

Up by 6:30 am, in the kitchen by 7 am. Table and butler trays set up the night before. Deliver butler trays by 7:30 am. Prepare, serve and clean up breakfast between 7 - 10 am. Check emails and return calls/messages 10-11 am. Laundry, ironing, shopping, gardening, errands during the middle of the day. Make sure rooms are ready for check in at 4 pm. Prepare hors d'oeuvres for Wine Down Hour 4-5 pm. Wine Down Hour 5-6 pm. Set table and butler trays; prepare own dinner 6:30-7:30 pm.

What is the most rewarding part of the job?

Meeting all our wonderful guests. We truly live our motto: Arrive as Guests. Leave as Friends.

Do you need to be a great cook to run a B&B?

You need to be a competent cook and able to pivot easily if a guest has a dietary issue/request.

Can one person run a B&B themselves?

At what point do you need help? One person could run a B&B solo if it is under 5 or 6 rooms, with housekeeping help. That is a must.

How do you deal with check-ins and check-outs?

We personally check in all the guests, give them a tour of the Inn and its amenities, get their order for their tray, double check about any dietary requirements and make sure they know the timing of Wine Down Hour, the trays and breakfast. We always make sure to say goodbye when guests leave, often helping with luggage and/or walking out to their car with them.

FORTY-THREE

Gaslight Inn

1727 15th Ave
Seattle, WA 98122

Bennett

**WHAT TIME DO YOU WAKE UP EACH MORNING AND WHAT DOES YOUR
schedule look like?**

6:00am get up start breakfast, we serve breakfast between
8:00am-10:00am, cleaning rooms till 3:00pm then check-ins
between 3:00pm-6:00pm then be available for helping guests
with dinner reservations, directions for entertainment and then
any late check-ins.

What is the most rewarding part of the job?

I get to live in and be a good steward to a one of a kind home that I would not be able to do if I wasn't creating this income to help with the financial end. I suppose also it would still be my ability to meet so many wonderful travelers that quite often become my dear friends!

Do you need to be a great cook to run a B&B?

Absolutely not, For 40 years I have offered only a continental breakfast. Being in a large urban city, my guests want to get out and explore, neighborhoods, restaurants, etc. I give them a great way to start their day and get on the road to explore or go to work. Rural areas need to provide full breakfasts since they are not in proximity to other great breakfast houses and are more of a destination.

Can one person run a B&B themselves? At what point do you need help?

Yes, I would say 2-4 rooms. I have always for 40 years just had 1 employee with my 9 rooms.

FORTY-FOUR

The Baker House Bed & Breakfast

65 W Market St
Rhinebeck, NY 12572

Sandra & George Baker

**WHAT TIME DO YOU WAKE UP AND WHAT DOES YOUR SCHEDULE
look like?**

If we have guests, we are generally up at 7 as breakfast is served
at 9. The shape of our day is largely determined both by the
number of rooms we have occupied on a given day and how
many are being turned over. As we do all our own cooking and
housekeeping, if we have all four guest rooms to turn over then
we will not get a break until the conclusion of Happy Hour, just
in time to feed our children dinner. If we have but one room
booked and those guests are spending another night, or will not

125

be attending Happy Hour, then we have no more obligation following breakfast than to briefly tidy their room.

What is the most rewarding part of the job?

There is satisfaction in creating a beautiful setting that pleases guests with welcoming, high quality accommodations that respects their intelligence and provides a respite from the crass commercialism of so much American consumer culture.

Do you need to be a great cook to run a B&B?

As breakfast is literally one half of the business name, if you can't do that well you are in trouble.

Can one person run a B&B themselves? At what point do you need help?

Perhaps if you have only one or two rooms and your house, and your guest rooms, are on the small side and spartanly furnished.

How do you deal with check-ins and check-outs?

We use an online booking system to streamline bookings and to charge deposits when booking a reservation and remaining balances easily at check out. The system includes automatic emails for reservation confirmation, check in times, and thank you after their stay.

FORTY-FIVE

Ambiance Bed & Breakfast

774 Lost Mountain Lane
Sequim, WA 98382

Dave and Corinne FitzPatrick

WHAT TIME DO YOU WAKE UP EACH MORNING AND WHAT DOES YOUR schedule look like?

Wake up 6:30-7:00am, depending on the time of year. Then prepare breakfast which is typically served at 8:30am. A lot of breakfast prep is done the night before to minimize the amount of work early in the morning.

What is the most rewarding part of the job?

As A Place of Peace, seeing people arrive and watch their jaw drop at our views, and then seeing their calm and peaceful presence after they've spent 2 or more days with us.

Do you need to be a great cook to run a B&B?

Corinne never focused on breakfast until we opened the B&B. While hesitant at first, she developed several key recipes and tested them on our family (while we all gained weight), and she has become an amazing breakfast chef. We do not provide any other meals.

Can one person run a B&B themselves?

It is possible if two rooms or less, but not recommended. It depends on how many rooms you have and how often you have to turn them over. The tough work is cleaning between 11am (checkout) and 3pm (an hour prior to check-in).

At what point do you need help?

Our advice would be 3 rooms or more.

How do you deal with check-ins and check-outs?

Check-in is between 4-6, and we will accommodate late check-ins. We always greet our guests at the door and complete registration and collect final payment before showing guests their rooms. All reservations are done through our web site or and Expedia-owned site, which all go through ResNexus (our reservation provider).

FORTY-SIX

The Australian Walkabout Inn B&B

837 Village Rd
Lancaster, PA 17602

Lynne & Bob Griffin
Owners

**WHAT TIME DO YOU WAKE UP EACH MORNING AND WHAT DOES YOUR
schedule look like?**

(Pre-pandemic on a typical day) I'm up between 6:30 and 7:00
am. Breakfast is almost always planned 3 or 4 days at a time, so I
make sure I have enough ingredients available. On weekends my
husband prepares the coffee, tea and the fruit course since he's
usually home. During the week I take care of all the meal myself.
After breakfast and check-outs, I clean the kitchen, walk the dog
and then start on rooms – either 'fluffing' for stay-overs or

turning rooms completely to get them ready for the next guests. A 'fluff' entails making the bed, exchanging any wet or dirty towels, tidying the bathroom, emptying the trash, and a general tidying up. After that I have enough time to make sure the common areas are clean, fill the fridge, bake some cookies and make sure there's hot water for tea. Check-ins starts at 3, and depending on what day of the week it is, I could spend until 10pm waiting for guests.

What is the most rewarding part of the job?

Probably being part of people's milestones. We get guests staying with us for honeymoons, birthdays, anniversaries, and other special reasons. We've had a few engagements, and my husband has even performed a couple of weddings at our property, though this isn't something we advertise.

I also enjoy 'paying it forward'. We've provided lodging occasionally for folks who need a little help. Whenever we've done that, it always comes back to us in wonderful and unexpected ways. It's fun to see what happens.

Do you need to be a great cook to run a B&B?

Personally, I don't think so. I do have several innkeeper friends who are culinary experts and put wonderfully crafted meals on their tables. I would not describe myself as a 'great' cook. We try to keep the items we serve within the parameters of a little more special than what folks might fix for themselves at home, but not so 'out there' that they feel intimidated by anything that might be put on the table in front of them. And for my own sanity, I try not to make things too complicated. A crabby innkeeper doesn't serve anyone well.

Can one person run a B&B themselves? At what point do you need help?

I have 5 rooms and do most everything myself. Bob takes care of the outside maintenance. I could not do both. I suppose it would depend on how many rooms you have and your occupancy. I think if you have more than 5 you'd probably want to get some help. Additionally, how breakfast is served also might necessitate getting assistance. I serve everyone together at 9am, but if you wanted to have an 'open seating' of an hour or more, you might need two people for that – one in the kitchen cooking and another serving and clearing.

How do you deal with check-ins and check-outs?

Again, I'll answer this question with pre-Covid information. Our check in is in between 3pm and 6pm. Occasionally guests need to get here before 3, which is fine with me as long as I know ahead of time and they actually show up when they say they will. Probably the most annoying part of the process is when people request to check in early, but then they get delayed for whatever reason and they don't update us. So we spend the entire day stuck at home waiting for guests who show up 6 hours after they've told us they need to be here.

FORTY-SEVEN

Chipman Inn

1233 VT-125
Ripton, VT 05766

Chris Bullock
Innkeeper

- "In Search of the Perfect Vermont Inn," New York Times Travel Section, July 18, 1982

WHAT TIME DO YOU WAKE UP EACH MORNING AND WHAT DOES YOUR schedule look like?

6:00 am. My schedule is full until between 9:00 pm and midnight.

What is the most rewarding part of the job?

Knowing that guests enjoy their stay and express their gratefulness for exceptional service

Do you need to be a great cook to run a B&B?

Great cook? Not at all, although being a great cook is certainly an asset. An exceptional personality and a willingness to be of service to people is your greatest asset.

Can one person run a B&B themselves? At what point do you need help?

I do not recommend it but yes, one person can operate an inn by them self. One person operating an inn by themselves is more likely to burn out quicker than two innkeepers partnering together. I operate the Chipman Inn by myself. But I am the exception; not the norm. I have 30+ years operations and finance and accounting experience with Marriott International and Hilton Worldwide at 15 different hotels in 12 different cities so I have a good idea of what to expect.

How do you deal with check-ins and check-outs?

I check in all of my guests with a brief tour of the inn, overview of amenities in their guest room, times for breakfast, explanation of cell phone usage and Wifi with a personal escort to their guest rooms. Like with check-ins, departures are handled efficiently and in a timely manner.

FORTY-EIGHT

Bay Tree Manor

4201 Seaford Road,
Seaford, Virginia 23696

Mark & Paige Stephens

- "One of the Most Welcoming" B&Bs in Eastern Virginia
2012, 2013 and 2014 by Virginia Living

- Coastal Virginia Magazine's Readers Choice Award in 2018
as Best Local B&B

WHAT TIME DO YOU WAKE UP EACH MORNING AND WHAT DOES YOUR schedule look like?

We wake up between 6 and 6:30am to make sure coffee is ready by 7am, we serve breakfast at 8:30am, we clean rooms after 11am checkout or earlier if rooms are available, we socialize and serve hors d'oeuvres between 4-7pm, we lock up when everyone is home and then go to bed.

What is the most rewarding part of the job?

The people we meet from all over the world.

Do you need to be a great cook to run a B&B?

No, but it helps. There are so many resources available just to make a great appetizer in the afternoon or just a simple baked good for breakfast.

Can one person run a B&B themselves?

Yes as long as you can simplify what you provide. At what point do you need help? When you offer a large breakfast to 10 or more guests. When you are very busy and can't clean all the rooms before the next guests check in, When you have a large property.

How do you deal with check-ins and check-outs?

We are very hands on because our B&B is our home. We require check in between 4-7pm but accommodate guests that have special time requirements. Check outs are much easier... we usually thank everyone after breakfast so they may leave at their leisure by 11am.

FORTY-NINE

Cedar Grove Inn

3636 Cedar Grove Rd.
Lebanon, TN 37087

Kim Papineau

**WHAT TIME DO YOU WAKE UP EACH MORNING AND WHAT DOES YOUR
schedule look like?**

6 am unless I have a guest that needs me earlier, two days a week
my 2 1/2 year old grandson arrives at 6:20 am and is here till
3:30pm. My husband Rich leaves for work at 7:15 after we feed
the chickens and if I have guest the bacon and coffee is on. I start
my regular job as an accountant for a CPA firm at 7 am or there
about (I work from home). On my breaks for for my lunch I take
care of guest, clean rooms or make beds, do laundry etc... I put in
at least 8 hours for work. After I make dinner and clean what

ever still needs to be done. I usually grocery shop on Saturday's. Sunday is family day and we have two son's, their family and a god-daughter and her family that joins us for dinner, if we have guest they are also invited and it happens very frequently. I also spend time baking when I have spare time.

What is the most rewarding part of the job?

Having guest tell me that they enjoyed their stay and reading their reviews.

Do you need to be a great cook to run a B&B?

No, but you should have a few things that you can perfect.

Can one person run a B&B themselves? At what point do you need help?

Everyone's situation is different, it would depend on how many rooms you have, if you can do things for yourself and if you work another job or not.

How do you deal with check-ins and check-outs?

We keep it very simple, we meet them at the door, we take them to see the room they reserved, give them the code to the doors and wifi password and we ask if they want to keep it on the same card as reserved with. Check out ends in a goodbye and see you again when you are in the area, sometimes a hug or two.

FIFTY

Walnut Canyon Cabins

503 Deer Rd
Fredericksburg, Texas 78624

Rhonda & Carl Rubadue

**WHAT TIME DO YOU WAKE UP EACH MORNING AND WHAT DOES YOUR
schedule look like?**

We wake about 8:00 since we do not prepare breakfast, we
supply local ingredients for the guests to prepare their own
breakfast in the comfort of their own cabin and enjoy their
breakfast in their private cabin or on the private deck and watch
the sunrise. Our day then goes to maintenance, marketing, usual
computer time, feeding the livestock and deer that roam the
property then call it a night between 8 and 10 depending.

What is the most rewarding part of the job?

Meeting interesting people, sharing stories, building relationships and receiving the comments from customers that really got to relax, unplug and unwind and that they cannot wait to come back!

Can one person run a B&B themselves? At what point do you need help?

There is NO WAY a single person could run an operation with 7 cabins as we have. Between our remote location, the laundry, the maintenance, the marketing, the accounting... We as a couple are thankful we have been able to secure a dependable housekeeper to do the majority of the cleaning of the 7 cabins.

How do you deal with check-ins and check-outs?

We love to meet our guests, during normal times we invite them in, offer a beverage, get a signature and share a story or two to get to know them and them to know us. Now we are practicing contactless check in and meet the guest as they roam the property. Checking out they guests can just leave the key in the cabin or come and share a thought of their stay before they leave.

FIFTY-ONE

Inn at Ellis River

17 Harriman Rd
Jackson, New Hampshire 03846

Mary Kendzierski

WHAT TIME DO YOU WAKE UP EACH MORNING AND WHAT DOES YOUR schedule look like?

What time we get up depends on how busy the Inn is. On a full-house day, we're up at about 6:00 am. John does the cooking so sparks up the ovens early. I do all the dining room set-up, breads and other foods for the first course (homemade granola, yogurt and fresh fruit cups). We start serving at 8:00 am. We have a breakfast sign-up sheet so we can stagger seatings. Our final seating is 9 or 9:30 depending on how many people are in the Inn.

Our guests are directed to any table of their choice. We offer coffee, tea and juice. We then offer our granola, yogurt, fruit and a choice of two breads. Once our guests have enjoyed some of those, we take a main order. Our main order is always an egg dish (frittata, crustless quiche. Etc.) or a sweet dish (such as Belgian waffles with bananas or a baked French toast). We offer our "famous" bacon or sausage on the side along with toast made from fresh bread from a local bakery. It is a full breakfast and most don't need anything until dinner!

Once breakfast and dishes are finished, we head to the rooms and common areas to clean.

What is the most rewarding part of the job?

It is hard to say what is most rewarding. I believe most of it is (though no one likes changing toilet parts). Each process every day is rewarding. We set up for breakfast. Lots of hard work goes into that. Then we serve it and have a bunch of happy guests. That is rewarding. Having piles of dishes that are all cleaned and replace is also rewarding as well as having guest rooms and common areas that have been used and in need of cleaning – once cleaned up and put back together again, they look wonderful. We are constantly able to witness the fruit of our efforts. I love to work out in the yard. There are three acres and every chance I get I am weeding, edging, trimming, etc. While breathing in fresh mountain air, after a strong workout doing landscaping, I can take a look at what I've done and be very happy about that – very rewarding.

Do you need to be a great cook to run a B&B?

No, I do not personally think so. I think it's important though. John, my husband, does most of the cooking and he is quite good at it though not professionally trained (most people think he is a trained chef) and Christine, our assistant innkeeper is a good cook and baker. That said, I think people can learn to cook but must be willing to serve high quality food and put great effort into it. If you can't cook but have the means to do so, hire someone that can cook well.

Can one person run a B&B themselves? At what point do you need help?

It really depends on the size. I think one person could probably handle a tiny one (4 rooms). Anything larger than 4 to 6 guest rooms., it is highly recommended to have at least one other person to help. To be an innkeeper, once must cook, clean, do marketing, public relations, working knowledge of Websites, in our case a bartender, money manager, etc. We have us (two owners), our assistant innkeeper and two housekeepers for a 22-room Inn. It takes quite a bit to cover an Inn this size to get it right. We could use more help but the money isn't there. Thankfully, John and I are still young and energetic enough to work very hard every day. We do it all.

How do you deal with check-ins and check-outs?

We have a main check in desk with reservation cards. We like to be present to check people in. We give tours of the common area to all guests, if they like. We offer to help with their luggage and show everyone to their guest rooms. Our cell numbers are listed in each room. We are in the building until 10 PM most nights. We have a late check-in process for those who arrive after hours.

Check outs – we like to personally check out each guest for a more personal experience. We like to know how their stay was, etc. Not everyone wants that. That's okay too. We have a basket at the front desk for people to drop off their keys.

FIFTY-TWO

Equinox Inn at Biscuit Hill

717 Colleen Dr
Canyon Lake, TX 78133

Darrin and Keith Hammons

**WHAT TIME DO YOU WAKE UP EACH MORNING AND WHAT DOES YOUR
schedule look like?**

We have 6 rentable rooms varying in size of 180-450 square ft in
nearly 5000 sq ft home. I get up 2 hours before breakfast serving
time, in the kitchen 1.25-1.5 hours before service. Plated
Breakfast / tray to room or patio 8:30-10AM. Clean kitchen by
11AM. Clean rooms as needed (average time 45 min-1.5 hours
depending on size), Laundry(up to 30 loads a week), computer
emails/marketing, check-ins 3-7PM, chef's choice breakfast prep.

I get out of the kitchen by 10PM. Hubby helps with some household chores, outdoor care, maintenance.

What is the most rewarding part of the job?

The incredible guests we have coming through our doors! And the many repeat guests we have generated over the last 3 years, that are like extended family!

Do you need to be a great cook to run a B&B?

No!! I have recipes that work well for my guests and environment. I thought I would make everything from scratch-reality is different! I tell guests that I try to cook/present more than what they would do for themselves on the weekend.

Can one person run a B&B themselves? At what point do you need help?

Depends on the size of the property and Innkeepers energy level. Before COVID- we typically had business 3-4 days a week (long weekend). So I was able to do most of the work, Keith worked in corporate America. Now we are 7 days a week, and Keith is here full time. I am considering some part-time housekeeping help next spring. And will be out sourcing the lawn maintenance next spring.

How do you deal with check-ins and check-outs?

We have an online reservation system that sends out conformation, reminder, COVID screening and receipt for payment a week before arrival. We meet guests at the door, sign in, then tour/explanation of the B&B on the way to their room, and additional explanation of room features. We do have a self check-in process that is rarely used.

Future plans?

Expand our intimate wedding venue, add additional rooms/cabins to have 10-12 rentable rooms, work smarter- not harder!

FIFTY-THREE

The Sedgwick House

7760 Main St
Hunter, NY 12442

Chris & Florentina

**WHAT TIME DO YOU WAKE UP EACH MORNING AND WHAT DOES YOUR
schedule look like?**

6 am to get breakfast ready and sometimes is working until last
guest is checked in even 9 , 10 pm - serving breakfast, cleaning,
check out and check in - just taking some breaks during the day -
weekdays less busy but weekend days are full days

What is the most rewarding part of the job?

Making guest feel special and eager to return sometime wishing to bring a group of family and friends

---

Do you need to be a great cook to run a B&B?

Not really, you can learn tricks along the way but be willing to anticipate and accommodate guests needs especially now days when people have gluten free or vegetarian requests

---

Can one person run a B&B themselves? At what point do you need help?

Not really, it has to be at least a team of 2, one in charge of daily operations and back of the house and another taking care of reservations, accounting, sales, marketing, website just my wife and myself. Depending on the size of the propriety might need to employ additional help for cleaning or repairs or even daily operations

---

How do you deal with check-ins and check-outs?

It's a touchless process now, just sending check in / check out details and using a website built in card processor for charges

---

FIFTY-FOUR

Pheasant Field Bed and Breakfast

150 Hickorytown Road
Carlisle, PA 17015

Kit & Robin
Innkeepers

**WHAT TIME DO YOU WAKE UP EACH MORNING AND WHAT DOES YOUR
schedule look like?**

This question made us smile. So, one of us is up between 5:00am and 5:30am (my Army career built that into me) and the other is up about an hour before our first breakfast serving (we serve breakfast between 7:00am & 9:00am). In general, our schedule is; breakfast (including prep and cleanup) from ~6:00 to 9:30am, from mid-morning up to about 3:30 we are doing general maintenance around the ten acre property (lawn care, working in gardens, facilities maintenance, etc), running around and shopping, and then check-ins are between 4:00pm and 7:00pm. The evenings we are usually hanging out with guests either catching up with return guests or getting to know new guests.

What is the most rewarding part of the job?

The guests!! We love meeting and getting to know new guests and reconnecting with our return guests. We have made some wonderful friends over the past eight years. It makes us feel good when they check out and we know they had a relaxing, comfortable stay and it's fun becoming a part of their life story.

Do you need to be a great cook to run a B&B?

A "great" cook? Not really. It does help to know how to make different breakfast dishes. My wife loves to cook and she makes it fun. Her dishes aren't that complex; however, she spends a lot of time in the plating of the food. She's an artist when it comes to plating because the guests see the food before they taste the food.

Can one person run a B&B themselves? At what point do you need help?

Short answer ... it depends. It depends how busy someone want so to be (remember we can control when and if we have guests). It depends on how many rooms they have. It depends on how much work they want to do. Yes, there are many innkeepers that run B&B's by themselves. They are typically less than 5 room inns (probably closer to 3 or 4 rooms), with minimal grounds keeping. If you get to the point where you're not having fun because you are always tired from working, then it's probably time to get help or reevaluate if being an innkeeper is still a good fit.

How do you deal with check-ins and check-outs?

Our check-in and check-out procedures are very simple. Since we have the majority of our guests' information from their reservation, including their payment method, our check-in consists of us welcoming them to the B&B (we always meet them at their car) and inviting them to relax. After that they are officially checked-in. Check-out is also very simple, we confirm their payment method, thank them for choosing to stay with us and wish them a safe trip as they continue their travels.

FIFTY-FIVE

The Owl's Perch

235 Squally
Robbinsville, NC 28771

Alice Lumbard

- The Owl's Perch opened November 2015 and have
earned the Airbnb "superhost" badge for 17 straight quarters.

- We joined Booking.com in July 2016 and have consistently
earned a rating above 9 out of 10

- We are proud to brag we have many 5 out of 5 star reviews.

WHAT TIME DO YOU WAKE UP EACH MORNING AND WHAT DOES YOUR schedule look like?

Typically our day begins at 7 a.m. allowing us time to get ourselves and breakfast ready to serve by 9 a.m. A turn over day requires cleaning, sanitizing, washing linens and stocking the essentials with the rest of the day maintaining the property. Constant attention to inquiries, bookings, promotions, correspondence to upcoming and post guests, etc is needed daily. All of these responsibilities are added to everyday life responsibilities.

What is the most rewarding part of the job?

Guest feedback on the craftsmanship of the cabin and our property and creek views.

Do you need to be a great cook to run a B&B?

Breakfast is not my preferred meal to eat! Ha! However, it's very rewarding to hear how much guests enjoy what I serve which is very basic.

Can one person run a B&B themselves? At what point do you need help?

One person could run a one bedroom B&B if they limit the availability and have computer skills to learn the different online platforms. More help in many areas is needed when your calendar is booked more than 50%.

How do you deal with check-ins and check-outs?

We live here so we greet our guests the majority of the time. Instructions on how to gain entry to the cabin are sent with directions if we are away at arrival time.

FIFTY-SIX

Inn on the River

205 SW Barnard St
Glen Rose, Texas 76043

Pamela Streeter

**WHAT TIME DO YOU WAKE UP EACH MORNING AND WHAT DOES YOUR
schedule look like?**

I get up around 530a - 6a on morning with larger numbers of guests so that we can get coffee out and breakfast ready for most people to eat between 8a-10a. We try to have coffee out around 630a-7a.

What is the most rewarding part of the job?

For me it is the dialogue that I have with guests where we learn about them and how staying with us makes them feel.

Do you need to be a great cook to run a B&B?

Breakfast is PART OF THE NAME, so while you don't have to be a great cook, you need to offer a great breakfast - it can be purchased from others - just make sure it is the best quality you can find of whatever you are serving.

Can one person run a B&B themselves? At what point do you need help?

No one can be in two places at once and yet that is what happens sometimes, you need a helper to either be cleaning rooms while you are handling guests or fixing something or answering phones. It probably could be done by one person but things will slip between the cracks....so hire people to help you if you are single and don't have a partner working with you.

How do you deal with check-ins and check-outs?

We are lucky to have a large enough living room that it is like a lobby, guests come to an antique desk and we begin the process of setting the tone of their stay by giving them info about the history, expectations of breakfast, where they can find refreshments throughout the day, the wifi info and encouraging them to use us as a concierge. When their stay if finished, most guests have become friends, so we have our goodbyes and take payment.

FIFTY-SEVEN

Manayunk Chambers Guest House

168 Gay Street
Philadelphia, Pennsylvania 19127

Mark F Jerde
Owner

WHAT TIME DO YOU WAKE UP EACH MORNING AND WHAT DOES YOUR schedule look like?

My alarm is set for 4:30am. I will start by turning on the oven and making my first cup of coffee. Pull out my premade doughs and batters to prepare for baking. I then gather the linens, dishes and flatware for the number of guests we are expecting for breakfast. Quietly. I make my way through the guest hall on the main level to our dining area in the parlor. Setting the table and filling the coffee station allows the guests to help them first thing when they rise with my being in their way. I can now focus on preparing their breakfast. Fresh baked pastry, bread and muffins are a must in our house along with fresh fruit selections and egg or other protein selections will also make the morning menu. Breakfast is served promptly at the requested time. It is important to have everything out once or served in courses to allow for you to spend some quality time with you guests. When breakfast is completed and guests return to their rooms to pack for their departure, it is time to clear the dishes and clean up the kitchen. I am sure to stay in the parlor so that I am available to help guests with bags and to say good-bye when they are ready to check out. Once they've departed it is then time to turn the vacant rooms to prepare them for the incoming guests. When completed I take care of any special requests that guests may have made prior. There are many duties to owning a B&B and your sharp organizational skills are vital to your success. Keep yourself available for your arriving guests to allow for a smooth check in process. Acquaint them with the parlor to make them feel at home and comfortable. Show them to their assigned room and familiarize them with their surroundings. I will offer any assistance that will help them to enjoy their experience to the utmost.

What is the most rewarding part of the job?

Having an exceptionally satisfied guest is my goal and greatest reward.

Do you need to be a great cook to run a B&B?

You should have some good cooking skills if you would like your guests to be happy. The old adage "the way to a person's heart is through their stomach".

Can one person run a B&B themselves? At what point do you need help?

I do it alone and quite successfully. So yes, it can be done. I enjoy all of the work by doing it all myself. From managing reservations and marketing to cooking and housekeeping to groundskeeping and public relations. You may want to hire someone when you no longer feel the joy from your daily tasks. I suggest when you hire someone to help you teach them everything you know to make them very valuable to you.

How do you deal with check-ins and check-outs?

With joy and excitement of your guests' experience.

FIFTY-EIGHT

7F Lodge and Events

16611 Royder Rd
College Station, TX 77845

Lisa Wantuck

WHAT TIME DO YOU WAKE UP EACH MORNING AND WHAT DOES YOUR **schedule look like?**

7am; Laundry room by 8:30am, office 9am, check emails post new bookings and send confirmations, organize the clean checklists for each cabin for the day, 10am to 11am - strip cabins from previous stays as they exit, laundry, 11am - greet housekeepers – advise them of any issues and the upcoming guests needs, laundry, 11:30am - possible morning Wedding Couple Tour, 12:30pm – 1:30pm inspect cabins as they are clean, set up breakfast baskets and final touches in each cabin before the guests arrive, 1:30pm - possible afternoon Wedding Tour, 2:30pm – set up more cabins, more laundry, 4:30pm – check emails, post new bookings, 5:00-6:30pm, check on laundry, lock up cabins not being used, lock up venue and office. Event/Wedding days are a whole other animal. And of course, this is not all done by me. I have a wonderful staff that I'd be totally lost without.

What is the most rewarding part of the job?

The job well done, the awesome reviews, meeting new people, our awesome staff and working side by side with my family (most days, LOL).

Do you need to be a great cook to run a B&B?

NO; we mostly do a continental breakfast. We do baking ahead of time and freeze it for the pastry box that we leave in each cabin (we're not the typical B&B with a cooked breakfast and guests love it that they don't have to go somewhere or meet at a certain time to eat)

Can one person run a B&B themselves? At what point do you need help?

Not with 8 cabins; it takes a village!

How do you deal with check-ins and check-outs?

Completely contactless. Guests arrive any time after 3pm and the key is in the door. Check out is by 11am and they leave the key in the cabin.

FIFTY-NINE

Snowgoose Pond Bed & Breakfast

10460 E Snowgoose Cir
Palmer, AK 99645

Jinks Greenstreet

WHAT TIME DO YOU WAKE UP EACH MORNING AND WHAT DOES YOUR schedule look like?

I get up at 6 am and head into the kitchen to begin preparing for 8:30 breakfast

What is the most rewarding part of the job?

A guest sincerely telling us they were so glad they found us and that a stay here was a perfect respite for them and just what they needed. We love it when guests truly feel at home.

Do you need to be a great cook to run a B&B?

Well, as I mentioned earlier, a lot of B&B's don't offer a home cooked breakfast anymore, so I guess you don't. But if you want to serve a hot breakfast . . . I don't think you have to be a great cook, but maybe a good cook and I think you have to enjoy cooking. Honestly, I wish I could just really pull out all the stops and do a super fun gourmet breakfast most mornings. But it's hard to do that not knowing who your audience is going to be from day to day and what their likes/dislikes are. So I walk a fine line between creativity and trying to make each breakfast special in some way --and--at the same time, being careful with ingredients that not everyone likes. Like I found a recipe for a beautiful brussel sprouts and bacon frittata the other day that I would love to try, but I probably won't because many folks just don't like brussel sprouts. As well, there are so many differing food intolerances and just preferences that it has gotten difficult, which is why I think many B&B's have given up on serving a hot breakfast.

Can one person run a B&B themselves?

Simple answer really -- it depends on the size. Ours is a small bed & breakfast, intentionally. I wanted to be able to cook and clean myself and not need to hire help. At what point do you need help? Well . . . I did break my wrist last summer. My husband does usually make his sourdough blueberry pancakes once a week, but he had to take over breakfast the rest of the week as well for me. He learned how to do some egg dishes that I usually make and did a fantastic job! I had a few friends come in and help with room changeovers. It was indeed a blessing to have friends I could call on for help when I needed it.

How do you deal with check-ins and check-outs?

Since we are small and do everything ourselves, we have a narrow check-in window from 4-9. It's hard to welcome guests very late at night since we get up early to cook breakfast.

SIXTY

The Parador Inn

939 Western Ave
Pittsburgh, Pennsylvania 15233

Ed Menzer

WHAT TIME DO YOU WAKE UP EACH MORNING AND WHAT DOES YOUR schedule look like?

I get up by 5:30 for my guests and to take my dogs for their walk before I have to start my breakfast duties. Many of my recipes I make the night before so the flavors have a chance to marinate like the one I'm providing.

What is the most rewarding part of the job?

By far my guests. When I shared on Facebook that my old guy had passed away, I got 400 condolences.

Do you need to be a great cook to run a B&B?

No but it helps. There's tons of good recipes on line that are easy. Quantify recipes you and your guests like in your own cook book.

Can one person run a B&B themselves? At what point do you need help?

Basically I do, I have one phenomenal housekeeper. Be sure to take care of your staff. I have a form welcome letter I put in the guest rooms with the guest's names. So she can hand write a personal note to them (instead of that tacky envelope with Housekeeping printed on it). My girls have walked out with $100 cash on some days.

How do you deal with check-ins and check-outs?

I have severe OCD and the check-in is very orchestrated. I give a tour of public spaces and tell them what they are welcome to. I then have a formal registration form that I get their mailing address (to the chagrin of OTA's like Expedia). My check-out is by 11 am and it says that in the personalized welcome letter I put in their room with the check-out time. I have very little trouble with this. Late arrival is huge, you could be missing tons of money by not accommodating this. It's relatively easy to set up with a lock box, and specific instructions on how to find their room. The welcome letter deals with the rest.

SIXTY-ONE

The Charleston Inn

755 N Main St
Hendersonville, NC 28792

Tommy and Kathy Crowder

WHAT TIME DO YOU WAKE UP EACH MORNING AND WHAT DOES YOUR
schedule look like?

Tommy and I wake up at 5:30 each morning so we can cook and serve breakfast to our guests. Breakfast is served from 8:00 am to 9:30 am each morning. We offer a full southern breakfast. Guests check out by 11:00 and check-in start at 2:00 pm. Our staff includes ourselves, our daughter Alicia, and a housekeeper. So, we all pitch in and help with every job. We serve an evening social hour that consists of complimentary wine and cheese every afternoon from 4:30 to 5:30. That is the time we best get to know our guest. We typically shut our front desk down around 6:00 pm and make special arrangements for our guests arriving after the front desk closes. We go home after that and then return around 9:00 pm to turn off lights and secure all doors. So, everyday is pretty full and about 12 hours.

What is the most rewarding part of the job?

Meeting new people and knowing that we provided them with a wonderful stay.

Do you need to be a great cook to run a B&B?

Well, that depends if you can cook. I cook for our Inn but have had a couple of chefs over the years. I personally find it easier to do the cooking myself because it is your reputation that goes out with every meal.

Can one person run a B&B themselves? At what point do you need help?

I personally think it would be difficult to run a B&B by yourself unless you have 4 rooms or less. It would be easy for a couple to run a B&B with 5 to 10 rooms but anything over that you would need help just so you couple have a couple of hours a week off. This is a job that you are definitely married too.

1. How do you deal with check-ins and check-outs? We do them personally at our front desk or if someone prefers a contactless check-in or check out we can arrange that as well.

SIXTY-TWO

Inn Of The Turquoise Bear

342 E. Buena Vista ST
Santa Fe, NM 87505

Dan Clark
Owner / Innkeeper

- 5 Bucket List Worthy Experiences in New Mexico

- TripAdvisor 2018 Certificate of Excellence & Hall of Fame

WHAT TIME DO YOU WAKE UP EACH MORNING AND WHAT DOES YOUR
schedule look like?

I do not live on our property. There is no owner's quarters at my Inn. I wake up at 5:00 am each morning. We serve breakfast from 7:30 to 9:30 am so we are preparing and serving breakfast until 10:00 am. Then baking afternoon treats. The rest of the day is being available to guests, answering telephone calls, checking rooms for check in or check outs, responding to emails, planning menus, shopping, etc. There's no shortage of tasks each day. It's the hardest job you'll ever love! We serve an evening wine reception from 5:30 to 7:00pm most days so it's a 12 to 14 hour day.

What is the most rewarding part of the job?

Providing hospitality to guests and meeting people. It's also satisfying to run a business with all that entails and to represent and share our beautiful city and state with visitors.

Do you need to be a great cook to run a B&B?

You need to be a proficient cook to start. You need to determine what your food vision is for your business and deliver that with consistency. The second B in B&B is breakfast....so it needs to be enjoyed and memorable. There's a sharp and long learning curve. However, it's only breakfast so it's not rocket science. We accommodate ALL food preferences, so learning about gluten-free, vegan, and other dietary preferences is a significant issue.

Can one person run a B&B themselves? At what point do you need help?

It's very hard for one person to run a B&B by themselves unless it is a very small "lifestyle" inn and you can control how you operate daily or seasonally. You need to be able to take time for yourself. The first year I acquired my 9 room Inn I did everything myself and it's a 100 hour work week. I hired an Assistant Innkeeper after my first year as we grew occupancy and I was able to cover the expense. Still, I work 70+ hours a week and my Assistant Innkeeper works 40+ hours and that is with additional staff.

How do you deal with check-ins and check-outs?

We service guests arriving and leaving in person. We offer contact-free check-in and check-outs at request. We accommodate early check-in and late check-outs whenever we can without additional hassles, restrictions or fees for guests whenever we can. It's part of the hospitality we provide. Typically we greet guests upon arrival, give them an orientation to our property, their room, breakfast, and other services. We answer any questions they have about their stay, our city, and things to do in the area. B&B's differentiate themselves based on this very personal service. We offer and provide concierge services to each guest as part of their stay.

SIXTY-THREE

The Yorkshire Inn

1135 NY-96
Phelps, NY 14532

Kathe Latch
Innkeeper

WHAT IS THE MOST REWARDING PART OF THE JOB?

Hands down it's the opportunity to meet and talk with people of diverse backgrounds and experiences! I have loved sharing time with all of our guests and learning about their lives, travels and interests over a cup of coffee or a glass of wine, as and having the opportunity to spoil them a little bit...I think we all need that!!

Do you need to be a great cook to run a B&B?

I think you need to enjoy cooking, so if you're not experienced in the kitchen, you need to learn quickly! Many guests come to bed and breakfasts because they've heard there is usually great food. That's a reputation every innkeeper I know tries to uphold. There are plenty of great resources out there if you don't want to create your own dishes, but you do need to enjoy preparing the breakfasts and presenting them well.

Can one person run a B&B themselves? At what point do you need help?

I would say it depends on the size of the B&B. I have four rooms now, two of which are family suites that sleep up to 6 people, but I started with two rooms. I have almost always run the Inn without outside help. It takes good time management and a little stamina, but a small Inn can be run by one person or a couple without hiring help. I think it also depends on occupancy. The times I have had outside help have been high season with almost 100% occupancy, and quick turnovers of rooms.

How do you deal with check-ins and check-outs?

This was a learning curve! We need to do in person check in, and when we first opened we just let guests check in when they were ready, which left us sitting around until all hours waiting. Our checkout time has always been 11:00 am. After a year or so, we put stricter guidelines in place for check in, now we are regularly available for check in from 3-6 pm, and if the guests need an earlier or later check in than this window, they need to contact us directly to make arrangements. When guests arrive the are issued keys for the front door and their room, these are turned back in to us the morning they check out.

SIXTY-FOUR

Black Creek Bed and Breakfast

430 N Riverside Rd
Highland, NY 12528

Dan & Brittany

**WHAT TIME DO YOU WAKE UP EACH MORNING AND WHAT DOES YOUR
schedule look like?**

We normally get up at 6-7 as we need to prepare a gourmet
breakfast daily. We constantly are working 7 days a week all
year.

What is the most rewarding part of the job?

By far the most rewarding part of this is, the friends and people we have shared time with.

Do you need to be a great cook to run a B&B?

Yes I believe you need to have great skill in the kitchen to cook for guest from all over the world.My family has a farming background. Everything was farm to table.

Can one person run a B&B themselves? At what point do you need help?

I guess it depends on the size. But I believe you really need at least two people.

How do you deal with check-ins and check-outs?

Check in is at 3 but we accommodate early as well as late check ins. Check outs are normally at 11:00 am but we don't push people out the door.

SIXTY-FIVE

The Gibson House Inn

419 S. Main
Kernersville, NC 27284

Darlene Pearson
Owner/Innkeeper

**WHAT TIME DO YOU WAKE UP EACH MORNING AND WHAT DOES YOUR
schedule look like?**

When we have guests we generally rise around 6:00. Mornings are busy and we try to keep afternoons and evenings light to accommodate guest requests and spending time with guests as they wish.

What is the most rewarding part of the job?

Meeting wonderful new people and hearing their stories

Do you need to be a great cook to run a B&B?

At least a good cook!

Can one person run a B&B themselves?

I think it takes at least two. At what point do you need help? Busy seasons require some help with the cleaning. Kitchen help is required when we have guests of guests for breakfast.

How do you deal with check-ins and check-outs?

We have set hours and do our best to accommodate requests outside of normal check-in/check-out hours. We have key-coded exterior doors, and we've done videos and pictures of the B&B for late arrivals to show them exactly how to get to their rooms.

SIXTY-SIX

The Dominion House Bed & Breakfast

50 Old Dominion Rd
Blooming Grove, NY 10914

Kathy

WHAT TIME DO YOU WAKE UP EACH MORNING AND WHAT DOES YOUR schedule look like?

Getting up early all depends on the individual morning, any where from 5:30 to 7:00 am.

What is the most rewarding part of the job?

The best part is the guests. You meet so many wonderful people from all over the world.

Do you need to be a great cook to run a B&B?

You don't have to be great just be able to follow a recipe. We only serve breakfast.

Can one person run a B&B themselves? At what point do you need help?

We only have three rooms so just my husband and I handle it. Hired help all depends on your amount of occupancy. We are mostly weekend business but in some areas you may have a lot of mid-week. We are also seasonal, very little winter business. It all location, location, location.

How do you deal with check-ins and check-outs?

We do in person check ins. There is not much to check outs, noon is our check out.

SIXTY-SEVEN

Letchworth Farm

8983 Oakland Road
Nunda, NY 14517

Richard & Daisy Trayford

- We are an Airbnb Superhost have a 9.6 rating with
Booking.com, 5* with Tripadvisor(etc)

- Recognized by New York dept of Tourism as one of the 15
most unique places to stay in NY.

WHAT TIME DO YOU WAKE UP EACH MORNING AND WHAT DOES YOUR
schedule look like?

6am - prepare for Breakfast.

What is the most rewarding part of the job?

Our guests - they are a wonderfully diverse group from around
the World. It's like the best of Rural America and a Dinner Party
in New York City!

Do you need to be a great cook to run a B&B?

No, but you do need creativity and passion and to be fully aware
that it's a 7 day per week commitment.

Can one person run a B&B themselves? At what point do you need help?

Possibly. My wife Daisy and I run a Farm as well as the
Guesthouse so we are always busy. If it were just the Guest
House I think no single person could do it for long (depends on
the size of course).

How do you deal with check-ins and check-outs?

We let our guests check themselves in - we simply leave a
welcome note explaining that we are Horse Farm and maybe out
working - its proved popular with guests as they tend to arrive

tired and want to go straight to a room. This has been especially important during the Covid era.

_____

SIXTY-EIGHT

Inn at Glencairn

3301 Lawrenceville Rd
Princeton, NJ 08540

Lydia Oakes
Chef and Innkeeper

WHAT TIME DO YOU WAKE UP EACH MORNING AND WHAT DOES YOUR schedule look like?

I wake up at 5:30 every day and I'm in the kitchen by 6:15 for my first breakfast seating at 7:30. I serve 4 different seating times so I'm busy with breakfast up through 10:30 with making, serving, and cleaning up between. After that, check out is at 11:00. I organize the housekeepers, run food and supply errands for the Inn and myself from 11-3:00p.m. From 3:00-5:00p.m. is our check in time so I'm here at the Inn; but we have gone to a self check-in process due to COVID. Prior to that and after, we have a hands-on check in where I greet guests and show them around the Inn before taking them to their rooms. Normally after 5:00p.m. I am taking care of my needs by relaxing, meeting friends out, or chatting with guests should they request it.

What is the most rewarding part of the job?

Knowing that I have met the needs of the guests who stay here. This means two things: 1) creating a delicious, talked-about breakfast including house made jams, yogurt, granola, breads, truffles, cookies. 2) Making sure the Inn meets and surpasses their expectations in cleanliness, friendliness, and interest. Guests let you know if you've done your job well.

Do you need to be a great cook to run a B&B?

No but being interested in creating delicious, interesting food is a huge reason people come back time and again. That's the goal of a B&B...return guests and spreading the word to friends. It always includes food.

Can one person run a B&B themselves? At what point do you need help?

Yes and no. I run all the B&Bs I've worked by myself but I've always had housekeepers. Some owners are more involved than others. The best partnership for me is an owner who handles the financial and marketing areas. Because I don't own the house, decisions about needed repairs or expensive purchases should be signed off by the owner.

How do you deal with check-ins and check-outs?

Currently we do self-check in for everyone due to COVID. The key to their room, house key, and a welcome letter are left for them at the door. They can easily navigate to their room where we have a 3-ring binder with more details including WIFI access, more COVID procedures, restaurants, things to do, etc. Pre and post COVID, I give them ideas on what to do, where to eat, etc. at check in. Then I leave them to enjoy their stay. I am always available by ringing a doorbell in the house. Checkouts are easy as we only need their key back. They have paid in advance so no collection of money is needed. People have their own schedules to adhere to so I don't want to be holding them up while trying to serve breakfast to other guests. Because I can hear them when they head toward the door, I have a moment to say goodbye even if I'm doing breakfast.

SIXTY-NINE

Bed and Breakfast at Oliver Phelps

252 N. Main St.
Canandaigua, NY 14424

∾

Karin Koepcke

WHAT TIME DO YOU WAKE UP EACH MORNING AND WHAT DOES YOUR schedule look like?

6am, sometimes a little earlier. I Set the dining room and get the coffee brewed, then I tend to a farm to table and organic 3 course breakfast which includes something sweet, something savory, fruit, juice and lots of love. Serving breakfast and cleaning up is done by 1030am. During breakfast I can chat with guests to make sure they are comfortable and answer any questions about activities they are interested in. The rest of the day I am taking care of small and large repairs around the house...or out and about enjoying the plethora of activities to keep myself in the know!! In the evening I finish any prep work for breakfast the next morning, check to make sure the tea coffee and water station is stocked, as well as put out baked good treats for guests.

What is the most rewarding part of the job?

The people!

Do you need to be a great cook to run a B&B?

HMMmmmmm I am told by my guests that I am a great cook and many comments are that they are coming back just for the food...so it definitely helps. I make sure that my breakfasts are loaded with healthy protein, plenty of fiber, and lots of great flavors! Guests often remark that they stay pretty full until dinner.

Can one person run a B&B themselves? At what point do you need help?

I do run it by myself. I have contractors who help with bookkeeping, cleaning, and lawn care, and major renovations. This way I can do the stuff I love like cooking, hosting, laundry etc...

How do you deal with check-ins and check-outs?

I have a booking system that keeps that simple.

SEVENTY

Black River Inn Bed and Breakfast

704 70th St
South Haven, Michigan 49090

Bob and Judine Kisielewicz
Owners/Operators

**WHAT TIME DO YOU WAKE UP EACH MORNING AND WHAT DOES YOUR
schedule look like?**

Typically, we serve breakfast at 9:30. We begin to prepare
breakfast between 7:30 and 8:00. We set the automatic coffee
maker in our dining area to go on earlier if guests indicate that
they are early risers. Many guests like to go for a walk before
breakfast on the Kal Haven Trail. Later, we change over rooms
if needed and run our errands for supplies. We serve little snacks
or refreshments in the afternoon and converse with our guests.

Sometimes, weather permitting, we will get a fire going on our outdoor patio and enjoy the evening with our guests.

Do you need to be a great cook to run a B&B?

My wife is an excellent cook and we rely on five or six dishes for breakfast. It is a team effort and we work together, but my wife does about 75% of the cooking. I chip in with potato pancakes on occasion from my mother's recipe. I am usually the first one down and start prepping. Our dishes are not gourmet, but good hearty, country style breakfasts.

Can one person run a B&B themselves? At what point do you need help?

We have only three rooms and it is just enough for the two of us. It can be stressful at times because we focus so much on the comfort of our guests and want them to have a great experience. We try to provide that little extra attention to detail for everyone. We are fortunate to have a great gal that helps us turn over the rooms after guests leave.

SEVENTY-ONE

Blue Dragonfly Inn

600 W. 18th St.
Cimarron, NM 87714

Erin Tawney
Owner

WHAT TIME DO YOU WAKE UP EACH MORNING AND WHAT DOES YOUR schedule look like?

I will prepare as much for breakfast the night before as possible, then I'm usually up at 6am to finish it up depending on what time our guests requested. When guests leave for the day, I will check bathrooms, supplies, and trash cans, making sure all is in order for their return.

What is the most rewarding part of the job?

The people, definitely! We always sit down (at least we did pre-Covid) with our guests over breakfast to get to know them, then we try to leave them alone the rest of the day to enjoy their stay in peace. Sometimes that's difficult as there are those folks whose presence you enjoy so much! We have met some of the most wonderful people from all over the US, and have remained friends with many of them. One guy from Philmont has a woodworking hobby and asked if he could make signs for the rooms (he incorporated our logo in each one!) and they're beautiful! We've received countless other anonymous gifts, and had the pleasure of meeting an angel who walks among us. No, really, she lives in VA, and is such an incredible spirit. Her nickname is Sunshine.

Do you need to be a great cook to run a B&B?

It certainly helps! You also have to be very aware of dietary restrictions. There are a lot of people who have allergies, or just weird stuff going on. I always ask, then get creative so someone can enjoy something they usually wouldn't be able to as well as not feel left out. Example: I will make biscuits and gravy for a person allergic to dairy using almond milk. Any extra steps you take make your guests feel loved and appreciated so don't overlook that. I don't usually do traditional breakfast food (unless there are children staying) as you can get that anywhere. The point of eating out is enjoying food you can't or don't make at home. Here in NM, we are the green Chile capital, and I will incorporate that where I can.

Can one person run a B&B themselves? At what point do you need help?

My Inn is small so I have no trouble running it myself with my husband's occasional help. During the summer can be a bit tricky with having to turn rooms quickly, but I have also set my check-in and check-out times accordingly so I have enough time.

How do you deal with check-ins and check-outs?

I will ask my guests for their approximate arrival time so I can be ready, and I usually take care of all business when they arrive so check out is very simple. Help with luggage, coffee to go, a hug if they want one, a wave and safe travel wishes.

SEVENTY-TWO

Mile Hill B&B

2461 Co Rd 21
Valatie, NY 12184

Maret Halinen

**WHAT TIME DO YOU WAKE UP EACH MORNING AND WHAT DOES YOUR
schedule look like?**

I wake up 6 a.m. usually and serve breakfast at 8:00. I am also a
realtor so it is a busy day.

What is the most rewarding part of the job?

The guests.

Do you need to be a great cook to run a B&B?

Well you need to be able to make few disses well. Most people want light and organic and gluten free etc. today and then there are the big eaters as well..

Can one person run a B&B themselves? At what point do you need help?

Depends the size of your B add B. it is allot laundry you need to chance after every person and clean. That can get old.

How do you deal with check-ins and check-outs?

Not a problem. You need to have times set for everything. I always contact people in advance

SEVENTY-THREE

Oak Creek Lodge

21575 Brady Rd
Bannister, Michigan 48807

Tracie Hymer

- **Michigan Lake Association.**

- **We are rated by Expedia 9.9 in guest reviews.**

WHAT TIME DO YOU WAKE UP EACH MORNING AND WHAT DOES YOUR schedule look like?

We get up at 6:45 or 7am and start with coffee/breakfast, the guest like to visit with us, cleaning, then office work, check ins, grocery shopping and prepping for the next day.

What is the most rewarding part of the job?

The thank you cards.

Do you need to be a great cook to run a B&B?

Yes.

Can one person run a B&B themselves? At what point do you need help?

We have 6 rooms, I think one person could do 2 rooms maybe, but any more than that you need at least 2, that have different skills. My husband fixes everything, and I do the office work. It is a great team.

How do you deal with check-ins and check-outs?

It took a lot of learning, but we charge people the day before arrival and then email instructions on how to get in, offering a touchless checkin.

SEVENTY-FOUR

Purple Martin Inn and Nature Center

194 East Freidrich Depot
Rogers City, Michigan 49779

Anne M. Kosiara

What time do you wake up each morning and what does your schedule look like?

730 to 8am and breakfast is served at 9am.

What is the most rewarding part of the job?

Hearing people say how much they love our place, and they will be back. Also, the guests who leave friends.

Do you need to be a great cook to run a B&B?

I believe so.

Can one person run a B&B themselves?

Not for long and not well.

At what point do you need help?

I think you need help and lots of it.

How do you deal with check-ins and check-outs?

We keep it personal and try to make people feel they are valuable
to us.

SEVENTY-FIVE

Moonshadow Bed & Breakfast

10249 Gibson Road
Hammondsport, NY 14840

Jeanette and Steven Harp

- Moonshadow has rated #1 in Hammondsport every year since 2015 on Trip Advisor.

- We have also been featured in Newsweek as a must-stay destination while visiting the Fingerlakes.

WHAT TIME DO YOU WAKE UP EACH MORNING AND WHAT DOES YOUR schedule look like?

We wake up at 7, have coffee/tea on at 7:30 and serve breakfast at 9. Once breakfast is done and our guests have left for the day we turn the rooms and do any chores/shopping that needs to be done.

What is the most rewarding part of the job?

We love the wonderful people we meet. We have become friendly with many of our guests, meeting up with them in their own towns and even staying the night at their homes! We have so many return guests who come 2-3, even 4 times a year it's like catching up with old friends.

Do you need to be a great cook to run a B&B?

Yes, I think so. You don't have to be innovative if that's not your thing but yes, I think great food is a huge part of the BnB experience. Have 10 great breakfasts you are comfortable with and perfect them, you don't have to reinvent the wheel every time. Also you really need to be flexible with dietary restrictions. Make sure you have vegan, GF, DF, and Veggie dishes readily available. I make sure to ask all guests before arrival if they have any restrictions so you aren't caught off-guard.

Can one person run a B&B themselves? At what point do you need help?

It's a hard job and I am very grateful to have a partner who is involved 100%. We split up duties; I clean the house and rooms, he does all of the bathrooms. We both cook. I take care of the garden, he does the yard work. This is our only job so that certainly helps!

How do you deal with check-ins and check-outs?

We try to be here for check-in's, but we are keyless so if we aren't here guests can check themselves in. For check out they are free to go, we charge the reservation 100% upon booking so there isn't any dealing with money on the way out. We are very low-keyed around here and prefer it that way.

SEVENTY-SIX

Knob Hill Bed & Breakfast

1105 South Dr
Flint, Michigan 48503

Diana Phillips

- 2017 Rising Star award from the Flint and Genesee Chamber of Commerce. This award honors a growing business beyond the startup phase, recognizes strengths related to growth, leadership, operations, innovation, and/or special work in the community.

- 2018 Art of Achievement Frontline Ambassador Award from the Flint and Genesee Chamber of Commerce and Genesee Convention and Visitors Bureau. This award recognizes a hospitality worker in a Genesee county hotel who provides outstanding service to guests staying at the establishment.

WHAT TIME DO YOU WAKE UP EACH MORNING AND WHAT DOES YOUR schedule look like?

We have no set schedule. Unlike most B&Bs, we check in guests by appointment and serve breakfast at the times our guests request.

What is the most rewarding part of the job?

The most rewarding part of operating a B&B is meeting all of our wonderful guests and providing our community with a lodging alternative.

Do you need to be a great cook to run a B&B?

You do not need to be a great cook although I am one. In fact, some local regulations do not permit prepared meals, only prepackaged foods are allowed. I haven't tested it, but I feel that as long as you provide a clean, comfortable environment and treat your guests as if they are the most important people in the world, serving cardboard would be acceptable.

Can one person run a B&B themselves? At what point do you need help?

Yes, one person can run a B&B but it is easier with help. Some B&Bs only have 2 or 3 rooms and most are not 100% booked. You need help when you can no longer handle the demands of the B&B without sacrificing the quality of your guest's experience.

How do you deal with check-ins and check-outs?

Our check-ins are by appointment and guests are personally given a tour of the B&B and shown to their rooms. Guests check themselves out.

SEVENTY-SEVEN

The Bentley Inn

694 Main Ave.
Bay Head, NJ 08742

Glenn Kithcart
Innkeeper

**WHAT TIME DO YOU WAKE UP EACH MORNING AND WHAT DOES YOUR
schedule look like?**

In season I'm up at 5am, showered and working at 5:30am until
7pm, 7 days per week (that lasts about 4 months). During that
time I am answering phones, doorbells, emails and texts,
overseeing my employees, cleaning, prepping and cooking
breakfast, planning, repairs, laundry…

What is the most rewarding part of the job?

People are my passion. They arrive ready to relax and have a good time and it is really good energy.

Do you need to be a great cook to run a B&B?

Not really. We have a griddle and cook to order from a 5 entree menu (our full capacity is 45 people). I learned to make omelets, eggs, waffles quickly. The hard part is feeding that many people in 1.5 hours… you need to be organized.

Can one person run a B&B themselves? At what point do you need help?

We have 19 guest rooms so you need lots of help to run this place. We have high school and college kids work here and they do a stellar job (again you have to be organized with cleaning checklists). I personally don't clean rooms but I do clean the common areas occasionally in season and frequently in off season.

How do you deal with check-ins and check-outs?

Pre Covid guests would ring the front doorbell and we would check them in, for check-out they don't need to do anything but many want to say good bye. With Covid we do everything with text and emails and have contactless check-ins.

SEVENTY-EIGHT

Blessings on State Bed & Breakfast

1109 W State St.
Jacksonville, IL 62650

Gwenn Eyer
Innkeeper

**WHAT TIME DO YOU WAKE UP EACH MORNING AND WHAT DOES YOUR
schedule look like?**

Don't steal it – I've always said if I write another book it will be
called "How to Run a Bed & Breakfast When You Don't Like
Getting Up at the Crack of Dawn." Tables are set the day before,
breakfast prep has been started, and I have lists and timelines to
help me manage my time. I still have a part-time job outside the
B&B, so I have to do that.

What is the most rewarding part of the job?

The relationships that result. We moved to a town that was unknown to us, 65 miles from our home of 25 years, to open the B&B. There was a reason we chose this town, but we didn't know anyone. We started building community relationships right away, and they're even strong today. We have strong relationships with our staff, and they "get" me and our mission. Yes, with only two suites I still pay part-time staff. (I still have a part time job outside to offset our expenses.) Our staff are like family. We all focus on meeting the needs of our guests, whatever our role. As we meet their needs, we develop friendships/relationships with them. It's all about the experience. Yes, we offer a beautiful, well-appointed inn. Yes, I'm a good cook. Yes, we have very high service standards. But it's all about the overall experience and relationship building at Blessings on State Bed & Breakfast.

Do you need to be a great cook to run a B&B?

Someone needs to be at least a *good* cook if you're going to offer a full breakfast. Our reviews demonstrate a high level of guest satisfaction with our breakfasts, but I use hacks and shortcuts to save time. I typically have help in the kitchen and often with service to the table.

Can one person run a B&B themselves?

It depends on your goals. At what point do you need help? I needed help from the beginning. If the majority of innkeepers burn out at 7 years, or whatever it is today, is it because they're all in 24/7? I had an exit plan from the beginning. I also identified areas of – maybe not weakness, but areas that I need help with. I was initially traveling much more with my job, and I knew that we need to take family breaks. (We adopted our fifth child a few years ago. 20 years younger than our last one, and deaf.) So… I needed to identify an inn-sitter so we could get away. Housekeeping is one of my top priorities, but it doesn't fill my heart with joy. So… I pay for housekeeping. I was diagnosed with breast cancer in 2016. When I finally posted it for my Facebook friends, I got comments like, "I can't cook, but I'll be glad to come in and greet your guests." "I cook a mean breakfast!" "I can come clean." People pitched in. My housekeeper became my sous chef, then I became her sous chef, then she became the chef and I sat around feeling miserable from chemo. I knew I could call in outside supports, as needed.

How do you deal with check-ins and check-outs?

Because I'm so focused on the experience and building relationships, I do it in person. However, we have a video doorbell and I'm comfortable with self-check-in, especially during the night. We just provide instructions in advance and leave a "light trail" to their suite. We ask the bride and groom to send someone in during the day to drop bags and pick up a key, then we leave a (fake) trail of rose petals to lead the way.

SEVENTY-NINE

West Hill House B&B

1496 W Hill Rd
Warren, Vermont 05674

Peter & Susan

- We are a member of Select Registry, Distinguished Inns of North America.

- Peter was presented with the Vermont 2019 Innkeeper of the Year Award by the VT Chamber. This award is designed specifically to recognize individuals who continue to demonstrate excellence in the operation and management of a Vermont bed & breakfast, inn, hotel or resort, and a commitment to the growth of the local community.

- West Hill House B&B was once again awarded the 5 star Certificate of Excellence by Trip Advisor in 2019 for the 9th consecutive year, and the 5 year "Hall of Fame" award for the fourth successive year. - The B&B was awarded the Trip Advisor "Travelers' Choice" Award in 2020 for being among the top 10% of properties globally. At an Awards Ceremony held on April 20th 2009 in the House Chamber of the Vermont State House, Governor Jim Douglas presented a plaque to Peter and Susan,
recognizing West Hill House B&B as a Vermont Green Hotel in the Green Mountain State. (One of the earliest to receive this recognition.)

- We have also been designated as a Green Leader at Gold Level by Trip Advisor.

WHAT TIME DO YOU WAKE UP EACH MORNING AND WHAT DOES YOUR schedule look like?

Getting up between 6AM and 7AM when we have guests. Preparing then serving breakfast, clearing up. Helping guests with their plans for the day. Having our own breakfast, housekeeping the rooms and preparing for new arrivals. Doing everything else that needs done that day! In the late afternoon helping guests with dinner plans, turning down rooms, then having our own dinner. If guests wish to, we chat with them after dinner.

What is the most rewarding part of the job?

Meeting interesting people from all over the world with all kinds of backgrounds and interests.

Do you need to be a great cook to run a B&B?

It definitely helps! Great breakfasts are what guests remember.

Can one person run a B&B themselves? At what point do you need help?

Doing it on your own is tough. Not only the work load and the diverse set of skills required, but also the benefit of mutual support and encouragement is key.

How do you deal with check-ins and check-outs?

Checking in means showing guests to their rooms and giving them a tour of the B&B. All the formalities are dealt with at the time of booking. Checking out is asking them to complete the online check-out, then waving goodbye!

EIGHTY

Mansion on The Mile B&B

228 N N East St.
Indianapolis, IN 46204

Tom Gaunt

Generally we wake up at 6 am to prepare a 4-6 course breakfast
often consisting of a fruit plate, soufflé, croissants, uncured
bacon and sausage along with an assortment of juices and
coffees. The time breakfast is served is chosen by the guests and
the guest's diet is always considered as well. Check out is at 11
am unless otherwise arranged. Upon leaving, rooms are cleaned
and prepared for the next guests arrival, usually set for 4 pm.
Meanwhile, laundry and dishes are done along with any yard

work, weather permitting. Guests may arrive for a later arrival when arrangements are made. Parking is provided in front of the B&B or on the property. Guests are given a set of keys and may come and go as pleased. Outside cameras and a ring door bell keep us informed should we be away from the property or in our residence on the third floor.

What is the most rewarding part of the job?

Besides sharing our lovely home once featured on the Home & Garden channel, the most rewarding part of our job is meeting people from all over the world as well as our home state and city. We have had wonderful experiences from a Chinese mother watching me make breakfast so she can do it for her son at home, to people attending the Gen Con Convention in costume and seeing the Indy 500 for the very first time. Then being a honeymoon sight or just hosting the grooms family, you share in their excitement and anticipation. Sharing the numerous sites and attractions as well as Indy's fabulous award winning restaurants is reliving the wonderfulness of our clean, safe city.

Do you need to be a great cook to run a B&B?

We found it was helpful to serve great food and pamper our guests with excellent service. We never experimented with a new recipe on a guest. We learned what the vast majority of people enjoyed or wanted and found it served us very well.

Can one person run a B&B themselves? At what point do you need help?

While I have experienced other B&Bs run by a single person, it was a very small operation and I suspected they did not enjoy it as much. Unless you are a larger B&B a couple or 2 people is much preferred from our experience. I did the majority of the work for several years until my husband retired. He was only available on weekends at first. It kept me very busy with three suites. Should a person get sick or have an emergency, and it does happen, it could be very difficult.

How do you deal with check-ins and check-outs?

We generally collect as they arrive. Check-ins are done in person by us as well as check-outs. Once checked in, we may slip out after they leave for supper or run an errand but we try to be very available when someone is in the home. If someone is staying for several days, you have developed a relationship. We have never had anything stolen. We do charge more than neighboring B&Bs and we tend to have a higher level of cliental. It tends to screen people for us. You can work harder or smarter. Being cheap you can makes lots of beds for $99 or few beds for $199 and make the same profit. We feel we can enjoy our guests more by working a little less.

EIGHTY-ONE

The Blue Horse Inn

3 Church Street
Woodstock, VT 05091

Jill Amato

**WHAT TIME DO YOU WAKE UP EACH MORNING AND WHAT DOES YOUR
schedule look like?**

Our schedules vary based on how many guests and staff
members we have on a day. We host 2 to 22 guests and serve a
three-course breakfast with 4 entrée choices each day. Guests
also choose a breakfast time from 8 am to 9:30 am. Some
mornings we get up at 5:30 am, and other days 7 am. Planning
and nightly prep (measuring out dry ingredients, or chopping
parsley, or baking muffins, etc.) is important for the breakfast
routine go smoothly.

What is the most rewarding part of the job?

Meeting guests! We have met so many interesting people! We love talking to our guests, but we are very careful not to hover or be intrusive… it takes a balance. We want guests to feel welcome, but we give them space to enjoy their get-away.

Do you need to be a great cook to run a B&B?

You need to be good at planning and prepping. You need to always test recipes before you put them on the menu. Only use your best recipes. Once you have a good rotation of recipes for your menu, repeat them. If you are smart about how you run your kitchen, you do not need to be a "great" cook, just a smart cook that knows the recipes he/she uses very well.

Can one person run a B&B themselves? At what point do you need help?

It depends on how many rooms/guests you have, and what you offer your guests. With our three-course breakfast and fresh baked goods every day, I could only handle about 2 rooms on my own. The larger your business, the more time you spend on the phone, on email, checking guests in and out, cooking, cleaning up from breakfast, general cleaning of common areas, caring for the grounds outside, and, finally, cleaning the guest rooms. With our 10 room inn (8,000 square feet not counting owner's quarters), 2 acre property, it takes one husband and wife team, plus five part time employees (one part-time cook for extra baking and to help on our busiest days, and three part-time housekeepers: one who works 3-4 days and two Sunday-only housekeepers. And, finally, one college-aged boy to help with projects and maintenance when he is home for summer and breaks.

How do you deal with check-ins and check-outs?

Check-ins can be tricky because sometimes guests do not realize that we do not have staff to man the desk. The guest might be the only check-in that day; when we first opened, I would sit at the desk for hours waiting for them, not knowing what time they would check in. I have become accustomed to contacting them ahead of time to ask about any special dietary needs, if they need dinner reservations, and to make sure they can find our parking lot. During that call, I also ask them for an ETA. Just asking for a simple ETA has made a huge difference in my day! Now I can plan my day accordingly. Check-outs are easy. Generally, just as we are finishing breakfast clean-up, I will hear people coming down the stairs with their belongings, usually taking a couple of trips to their car before turning in their key and saying good-bye. Good-byes are important, and it is also a chance to make sure the guest enjoyed their stay, and to invite them back to see us again.

EIGHTY-TWO

Oft's Bed and Breakfast

11523 N 156th St.
Bennington, Nebraska 68007

Gordon and Linda Mueller

- **Property is listed on the: "National Register of Historic Places".**

- **"Hidden Treasure Award" from the Nebraska Heritage Program**

- **Recently featured in: "Luxurious Living Magazine"**

- **Featured in: "Only in Nebraska".**

- **Identified as one of the "Romantic Places to Stay" in Nebraska.**

WHAT TIME DO YOU WAKE UP EACH MORNING AND WHAT DOES YOUR schedule look like?

Morning starts at 6am with a cup of coffee, check messages and then start breakfast.

What is the most rewarding part of the job?

Socializing with our guests and return customers.

Do you need to be a great cook to run a B&B?

No but it helps.

Can one person run a B&B themselves?

Yes, Airbnb has proven that but you need a backup incase of illness.

At what point do you need help?

Depends upon the individual but a good rule of thumb is one person for each room. My wife and I handle 3 rooms and it keeps us extremely busy.

How do you deal with check-ins and check-outs?

Prior to the pandemic, we met guests at their car to welcome them and help with their luggage and then give them a tour of our home. Checkout, guests are given a sack of our homemade cookies and a warm farewell.

EIGHTY-THREE

Cucharas River Bed and Breakfast

90 Cuchara Ave
La Veta, Colorado 81055

Gaylene Smith

WHAT TIME DO YOU WAKE UP EACH MORNING AND WHAT DOES YOUR schedule look like?

I typically get up around 6:00 a.m. to begin breakfast so that it is served at 8:00 a.m. I do cleaning, laundry, etc. until around noon. Then I have some time to enjoy or do yard work. Check in guest in the evening. It is for sure a full day, but one that is very rewarding.

What is the most rewarding part of the job?

Being able to visit with so many different people and sharing my dream with them.

Do you need to be a great cook to run a B&B?

No just get really good at a few items and do them great.

Can one person run a B&B themselves?

Yes, as I do, however, I do have a great cleaning company that I hired to do the rooms.

At what point do you need help?

When you work too much.

How do you deal with check-ins and check-outs?

I live on the in a cabin connected to the B&B so I am here to greet my guests most evenings and I am the one cooking and serving breakfast so I do the check-outs.

EIGHTY-FOUR

Birchwood Inn

7 Hubbard St.
Lenox, MA 01240

Tom Johnson and Debbie Lancaster
Innkeeper/Owners

**WHAT TIME DO YOU WAKE UP EACH MORNING AND WHAT DOES YOUR
schedule look like?**

Debbie and our cook typically make it to the kitchen between 6:00 a.m. and 6:30 a.m. I follow shortly behind and prepare the tables and coffee. Pre-Covid we served breakfast at either 8:30 or 9:30 depending on the guest's preference. We now serve breakfast at almost any time the guest requests, so have had everything from 7:00 to 10:00 breakfasts to allow for maximum social distancing. Clean up follows and is usually wrapping up by 11:00. In a normal busy summer, housekeeping would come in around 8:30 to make over the rooms for the guests eating at 8:30, then move to the 9:30 rooms, then move to the checkouts that leave at 11:00 in preparation for that day's check ins that start arriving at 3:00. Every once in a while a plane is late or the guest is delayed for whatever reason and I, the innkeeper, have had to wait up to check them in. Typically, I can run errands or tackle repairs before check in time and can have dinner at a usual hour, watch a little TV and turn in before 10:00 p.m.

What is the most rewarding part of the job?

People are fascinating. The best part is to engage them and listen to their stories, hopes and experiences.

Do you need to be a great cook to run a B&B?

We have one and I can't imagine what it would be without one. Other innkeepers I have spoken to can get by providing a continental buffet for breakfast, but they also cannot charge the same as we do. I have had guests come here specifically looking for the better breakfast experience. The cooking is almost always mentioned in guest reviews.

Can one person run a B&B themselves? At what point do you need help?

If the person wants to cook every meal, wash every dish, make every bed, clean every room, fix every broken blind, unplug every clogged toilet, get up early and stay up late, then yes one person can run a B&B by themselves. That formula might work with three or four rooms maximum and I would expect the person to wear out quickly. Seasonality of the B&B is significant in the formula. If the season is only three months and then it is quiet the rest of the year, a single person will have better chances of maintaining some sanity. If the person is not an expert at everything then they need help to fill in the gaps. Decide what you like and don't like and then determine if you can find another person and afford another person to fill in for your deficiencies.

How do you deal with check-ins and check-outs?

I go out and meet the check-ins at their car, discuss whether they've been before to the area, to the inn, what they want to do, indicate what the weather will be and chit chat for a few seconds or longer if it isn't busy at the moment. I offer to help with the bags, or just grab the one that looks the biggest. Once inside the inn, I provide maps of the town, review the restaurants and shops then discuss other attractions based on what they have indicated they hope to do. I walk them through the downstairs, explain breakfast and sign them up for a time to eat. We discuss dietary restrictions if any, such as lactose intolerance or celiac disease, and we discuss their preferences, such as vegetarian, vegan, cream or milk for coffee, etc. They then follow me to the butler's pantry where we discuss the afternoon sweets, coffee machine, tea, and use of guest dishes, wine glasses and bottle openers.

EIGHTY-FIVE

Nola's Onekama Hideout

8195 5th St.
Onekama, Michigan 49675

Nola Teye
Owner/Operator

FIRST BRIEF HISTORY:

I worked in corporate America for most my life, then something changed during the dumbing down of America, they no longer valued the workers with knowledge and good work ethics. They were hiring workers who did nothing but play on their phones, and did FB on their computers. Paid them more and left the rest of us to do all the work for less pay. That did not sit well with myself, so I started thinking "a lot"

I have a big love for people and my gifts are service, so I started by helping 3 beautiful ladies with light housekeeping, small maintenance, when I realized they were lonely, very lonely. We became the best of friends and I loved them all very much in their own special uniqueness.

This was not enough income to meet my expenses, so I decided to pack it up and move back to Michigan where my grandchildren were and my aging parents. So I ended up in Newaygo, Mi then when walking one day I saw a sign for innkeeper at the local B&B, and I remembered the words of one of these dear women I helped. Nola you would make a wonderful Bed & Breakfast owner. I knew nothing of what it would take, so I applied and got the position. I wouldn't have to find a place of my own, I would live on the property and run it.

I woke every morning at 5:30 and made breakfast for 6 to 20 persons each morning, at first it was a buffet breakfast as they had always done, they i found more and more had health issues, vegan, whatever the issue or desire, I started making single plates for each quest with whatever they wished for breakfast. A little hairy at times, but always given grace for my efforts. People who come to Bed & Breakfast are different from the ones who go to Hotels, Motels. They want interaction, some are lonely, some curious, some just enjoy life and people and want to know all about you.

I would serve anything from Crepes, Pancakes, Eggs (any way), bacon, sausage, yogurt, oatmeal, Hash Browns, and fresh bakery made myself.

I maintained the lawn, flower beds, snow shoveling, snowblowing, cleaning, bedding, dishes, cooking. They were long days, but oh I learned so much and knew I loved this lifestyle enough to purchase my own.

I worked at Newaygo B&B for one year to the day, they moved to Onekama, Mi to run my own and be near my parents. What I learned from here is just be yourself, be genuine.

I looked one day and found my property, it took months to buy because the Village here does not allow bed and breakfasts here in the village. So I found a common friend here to help me and I found a way around. I am called a Vacation Rental, ran as closely as a Bed & Breakfast as possible.

I do most of the work here, lawn, maintenance, cleaning, booking, greeting, etc. "all of it" except for plowing drives, and some mechanically I can't figure out. I work most days from 6 am till 10-11pm. I love every second when busy with family and friends.

What time do you wake up each morning and what does your schedule look like?

6 am, get myself ready, coffee and bakery by 7am, yard work, or sit and wait for a quest to awake and greet them to find out their days adventures and upon arrival hear all about it. Dishes, clean house, clean rooms as quest check out, laundry, mow lawn, clean pool, weed flower beds, paint, then in the evenings, we cook, if have enough who ever want to join in can, sit around a camp fire and enjoy conversation, greet and check in quests. Late arrivals also a lot during summer.

What is the most rewarding part of the job?

The guests, the returning guests, all of my new friends and family.

Do you need to be a great cook to run a B&B?

No, just have to have love for people.

Can one person run a B&B themselves?

I have run Newaygo B&B by myself, and I have done it alone here for 2 years, been hard work, but it is mine. I am ready next year to have a part time cleaner so I can enjoy more guests.

At what point do you need help?

That depends on you, I am a hard worker, I can go all day and run circles around people, some can't. I can do it alone, a couple should always be able to do it together easily. When you start feeling like your life isn't yours any more or you feel resentful about doing what you do, then find someone who will love your quests and build your business.

5. How do you deal with check-ins and check-outs? I have a beautiful Grid (Resnexus) if let's me know when most quests book, some do call in and book, my comebacks are calling and doing it themselves on my website. Expedia, Hotels.com, booking.com, AirBnB come on to my grid by direct connect with Resnexus. You have to be paying attention to your grid all day unless you know you are all booked up and nothing else can come through, but even then you may have a cancellation come through.

EIGHTY-SIX

Ashley Manor

3660 Main Street
Barnstable, MA 02630

Keith and Allison McDonald
Proprietors

- **Trip Advisors Travelers Choice Award for 2020. Top 10%
of Hotels worldwide**

- **AAA Best of Housekeeping for 2020**

WHAT TIME DO YOU WAKE UP EACH MORNING AND WHAT DOES YOUR schedule look like?

We usually get up at 7am for breakfast service beginning at 8:30. Our daily schedule from there changes everyday as the day unfolds. Allison and I run the place from top to bottom so it is not unusual to work 15 plus hours a day during the high season.

What is the most rewarding part of the job?

The most rewarding part is the sense of pride we feel about our historic home and business. Knowing we made the right decision is very fulfilling.

Do you need to be a great cook to run a B&B?

Someone needs to have skills in the kitchen. Breakfast is in the title so it better stand out.

Can one person run a B&B themselves? At what point do you need help?

I don't think any one person could run a successful B&B. Way too many moving parts. Number of rooms, occupancy rates, size of property and services provided all play a part when it comes time to hiring help.

How do you deal with check-ins and check-outs?

We have moved to a touchless check in and out system but regardless it is always in person with a warm greeting and a fond farewell.

EIGHTY-SEVEN

Irving House at Harvard

24 Irving Street
Cambridge, MA 02138

Rachael Solem
Owner and General Manager

- **Board Member, Cambridge Local First**

- **Board Member, Harvard Square Business Association**

- **Board Member, Massachusetts Lodging Association**

- **President, Cambridge Hotel Association**

WHAT TIME DO YOU WAKE UP EACH MORNING AND WHAT DOES YOUR **schedule look like?**

I do not have operational responsibilities any more in this 44 room guesthouse. I can work whenever I like. I work Sunday-Tuesday on site, and work at home other days. My hours are generally 7-3 when I go to work.

What is the most rewarding part of the job?

Hearing from the guests, in person or by email.

Do you need to be a great cook to run a B&B?

No, but you need to have SOMEONE create great food. We have kitchen staff as well as engaging local bakers.

Can one person run a B&B themselves?

Depends on the number of rooms. 2-3 can be done by one person, but that person NEVER gets a rest.

At what point do you need help?

More than 4 rooms and if you ever want a break.

How do you deal with check-ins and check-outs?

We have enough rooms (44 in one house, another 11 in a house up the street set up for long-term stays) to justify desk staff 24/7. This is very helpful for all.

EIGHTY-EIGHT

The Wayward Traveler's Inn

2398 N. Singleton Avenue
Mims, FL 32754

Tina Adamson

- For the years 2019 and 2020 we have received a 9.6 rating
(out of 10.0) from Hotels.com for "Most Wanted Award".
This is based on overall customer ratings.

WHAT TIME DO YOU WAKE UP EACH MORNING AND WHAT DOES YOUR schedule look like?

We are usually up by 7:00 and begin putzing about. We have a Continental Breakfast set up and tell people when they're checking in that we don't mind them helping themselves to anything. We have items that are easy to grab and go with if they have an early morning.

What is the most rewarding part of the job?

We enjoy hearing others' stories of their adventures and what they do and where they live. We hear over and over what a relaxing home we have and that makes us happy to accommodate people and make them comfortable.

Do you need to be a great cook to run a B&B?

No, we do a Continental Breakfast and don't cook anything. We keep fruit and fruit juices, nice muffins, pastries, cereal and almond and regular milk, cereal bars, coffee pot (Keurig) and teapot with assorted teas as well as frozen breakfast sandwiches that can be microwaved by the guests.

Can one person run a B&B themselves? At what point do you need help?

One person can run it if they are not responsible for all of the cleaning and maintenance as well. We work as a team and have been doing everything ourselves and that works, but just one or the other of us would not be able to keep up with everything by ourselves.

How do you deal with check-ins and check-outs?

We have a "preferred"check in time of 3-6 pm and ask guests when they think they will be arriving. We do allow a little earlier if they are expected at a wedding at 4:00 or something else that we can accommodate without inconveniencing another guest. One or the other of us makes sure to be here to greet them, show them around, give them access information and make them comfortable, checking to see if they need anything before we kind of disappear into the background.

EIGHTY-NINE

Main Street Bed & Breakfast

208 E Main St
Glasgow, KY 42141

Cherie Vaughan
Owner/Innkeeper

WHAT TIME DO YOU WAKE UP EACH MORNING AND WHAT DOES YOUR schedule look like?

I wake up about 7:00am, breakfast is served at 8:30am. Guests check out by 11:00am and check in after 3:00pm.

What is the most rewarding part of the job?

Meeting all of the interesting people.

Do you need to be a great cook to run a B&B?

It definitely helps!

Can one person run a B&B themselves? At what point do you need help?

I have 5 rooms and run it by myself. More rooms would probably require more help.

How do you deal with check-ins and check-outs?

I'm flexible with times. They just have to contact me to make arrangements.

NINETY

Beall Mansion An Elegant Bed & Breakfast Inn

407 E. 12th St.
Alton, IL 62002

Jim & Sandy Belote

- "National Geographic Map Guide Destination"

- "TripAdvisor Hall of Fame" Award Winning Property

- "50 Best B&Bs in America" -The Daily Meal

-" USA Top 100 Gold Inn & B&B" Award Winning Property

- "Top 30 Bed and Breakfast" -Midwest Living

-" Best Illinois Bed & Breakfast" -Illinois Magazine Readers Poll

- "Top 25 Romantic Getaway" -BBW Magazine

- "Top 3% of accommodations worldwide for customer satisfaction" -HotelsCombined

---

WHAT TIME DO YOU WAKE UP EACH MORNING AND WHAT DOES YOUR schedule look like?

Usually about 6:30 a.m. but it depends on what is on the schedule for the day. I take care of the business side of things which usually begins with checking e-mails and for any overnight online bookings. After that, each day is different - great if like me you like variety. My wife is in charge of day to day operations which means either supervising or doing everything it takes to be a homemaker. The difference is that instead of being homemaker for family and self, innkeepers are homemakers to their guests (and the pay is better too).

What is the most rewarding part of the job?

The lifestyle. We get to live in a house that we couldn't otherwise afford, don't have to dress for the weather worry about rush hour traffic, get to work in a clean, beautiful surroundings, and have the best clientele any business could possibly ask for.

Do you need to be a great cook to run a B&B?

It depends on your clientele. Some b&b's do a simple continental breakfast – no cooking skills involved. Others provide country style breakfast – some cooking skills required.

Still others offer gourmet breakfast – excellent cooking skills required. In our case, in non-COVID times, we offer guests continental and gourmet breakfast options each priced accordingly.

Can one person run a B&B themselves? At what point do you need help?

It depends on the size of the property and occupancy rate. When you can't keep up or you are so busy it's no longer fun to do you need help.

How do you deal with check-ins and check-outs?

We offer guests a choice of either personalized check-in and complimentary tour of the property or self check-in - whichever they prefer.

NINETY-ONE

Serenity Hill Bed and Breakfast

3600 MAMMOTH CAVE ROAD,
BROWNSVILLE, KY

Tina Burr

FROM THE OWNER:

I am Tina Burr, the owner of Serenity Hill Bed and Breakfast in Brownsville, KY. I got my start in the B&B industry was a fluke. My husband and I talked about owning our own B&B one day, but time just never seemed right. One day my husband and I were talking when we decided we wanted a bigger house, so we went looking and found this home we liked. We called a realtor and gave her what we were looking for. One day she called and told us about a house for sale that we might like. We scheduled a viewing. As soon as I drove up the driveway, I fell in love with the view, and everything I was looking at. We walked up to porch and entered the house. I was blown away again by what I was shown. I was in love with the house and imagined us living there. While speaking with the owner we found out we were at a fully open and running B&B. I told my husband I wanted house. He said we can close the bed and breakfast and live in it as a home. I said let's try running the business. My husband said he couldn't help because he already had a job. I said I will do it and if I couldn't do it or liked running it we could close it up. I have never been or even ran a business before. I was nervous about doing so. I was so nervous and scared at the same time upon meeting and greeting my first ever guests, not knowing anything about what I was doing or supposed to do, but I decided to just be myself and sink or swim on my own. I ran with how I wanted to run my business and have loved every moment of what I do. I treat everyone the way I want to be treated. Now after two years, I still love what I do and all the people I have met along the way. Everyone who stays here is now family or forever friends. I thank God everyday for my wonderful life. I am a very lucky person to also have such a loving and supportive husband. I have the best of two worlds. There isn't a day that I don't have a smile on my face because I love what I do. Guests are more relaxed when they see how much you enjoy what you do. This is not a job to me at all. This is my passion. Serenity Hill Bed and Breakfast is know for its location to Mammoth Cave National Park in Cave City, KY. Serenity Hill Bed and

Breakfast is one mile from cave, many trails, as well as many other things to do and places to see We try and give suggestions on things to do while in the area as well as to suggestions on local places to eat. All my guests either find us via referrals, online searches, or on website of ours. We use previous guest referrals, advertise through Mammoth Cave, national corvette site, resnexus, booking, convention centers, just to name a few. I honestly believe my bed and breakfast speaks for itself by all the wonderful reviews it receives, as well as all my guest referrals. The most rewarding part of running my bed and breakfast is all the people I get to interact with. I start my day by getting up at 6am every morning and by 6:30am all breakfast beverages are set out. A huge country breakfast is served at 8am. After breakfast we clean and sanitize rooms to get ready for next guests. Then I have rest of day to do what I need to do, whether that be paying bills, laundry, etc. Being a good cook or having a good cook will be a plus in this line of work. Always remember to love what you do and all your hard work will pay off tremendously. One person can run a 5 room or less B&B if they want to but not if they don't have the love or passion to do it. If you have a bigger B&B, you are definitely going to need help. If you are busy with current guests and have more check-ins immediately following as well as check-outs all at same time can be a little hectic at times but if you stay true to yourself and stay patient, all will work out. Sites like Airbnb have very little impact on B&B's. I have been known to get some Airbnb guests stay with us from time to time. We all work with one another to make each other successful. It's not a competition, because there is plenty of room for everyone. We have awards for being a porch partner with a mothers rest, certificate of excellence from corvettes as well as trip advisor, a 10 rating certificate from booking.com, just to name a few our reviews and guest referrals are our best marketing avenue. Serenity Hill Bed and Breakfast is open year round from 24 hours a day.

NINETY-TWO

Sylvan Falls Mill B&B

156 Taylors Chapel Rd
Rabun Gap, GA 30568

Linda Johnson

Certified Green establishment 2015 to present

WHAT TIME DO YOU WAKE UP EACH MORNING AND WHAT DOES YOUR schedule look like?

I am an early riser, my partner is the late night contact. Wake, make coffee, set for breakfast, chat with guests, check out, clean, check in guests, chat, sleep.

What is the most rewarding part of the job?

Seeing the stress disappear from guests over the time of the stay.

Do you need to be a great cook to run a B&B?

No, you have to enjoy being in the kitchen though

Can one person run a B&B themselves? Yes At what point do you need help?

I would say that over four rooms at over 50% occupancy if you are over 50 years old

How do you deal with check-ins and check-outs?

Have set time but will work with individuals to make adjustments. Communication is the prime factor.

NINETY-THREE

Kilgore Mountain Hideaway B&B

3302 Lariat Rd
Island Park, Idaho 83429

**WHAT TIME DO YOU WAKE UP EACH MORNING AND WHAT DOES YOUR
schedule look like?**

---

7 or 8 since I don't have to cook breakfast. First thing I do is
check emails, texts that came in during the night. Go up to

mingle with the guests. I usually have housekeepers so spend my day answering phone calls, making reservations, updating websites, etc. But I often have to clean and make beds too. It's a VERY busy job because I also own a hostel!

What is the most rewarding part of the job?

Meeting all the awesome people that come through! :)

Do you need to be a great cook to run a B&B?

I do a continental breakfast because Idaho Laws for cooking meals are ridiculous.

Can one person run a B&B themselves? At what point do you need help?

If the B&B was small enough they could run it by themselves if they want to work EVERYDAY! haha If you have more than 6 rooms or want days off then you definitely need to hire someone to help with the housekeeping.

How do you deal with check-ins and check-outs?

I or a host is at the bed and breakfast in the evenings when guests arrive. They are given a tour of the kitchen, where to find breakfast foods, and then shown where all the common areas in the lodge are, then shown to their room and given the code to their door. They are also told the house rules and wifi information during this time.

NINETY-FOUR

Surf Song Bed & Breakfast

21 Officers Row
Tybee Island GA 31328

Jeremy

WHAT TIME DO YOU WAKE UP EACH MORNING AND WHAT DOES YOUR schedule look like?

6:30-7:30 - Wake up, get ready, head to the kitchen

7:30-8:30 - Make breakfast

8:30-9:30 - Serve breakfast, chat with guests

9:30-11:00 - Clean kitchen, clean the dining rooms, guest checkouts

11:00-3:00 - Clean and freshen guest rooms

3:00-6:00 - Guest check-ins

6:00-7:00 - Eat dinner, clean up

7:00-9:00 - Prep tomorrow's breakfast

Of course, you can't schedule when the phone rings, when a guest needs attending, or when the toilet breaks.

What is the most rewarding part of the job?

For Megan, it's the creativity of meal prep. For me, it's maintaining the beautiful home and grounds.

Do you need to be a great cook to run a B&B?

Absolutely not. I've hard of B&Bs that don't serve breakfast. Which, you know, should be illegal. Some offer store-bought bagels and OJ. I would be sorely disappointed with either. But even if you're not a gourmet (Meg and I aren't) you can still scramble eggs and fry bacon. Most guests aren't looking for elaborate. They're just happy they don't have to cook. If you can beat cold cereal, you're good.

Can one person run a B&B themselves? At what point do you need help?

This depends on the Inn and the Innkeeper. Meg and I run a 5 room inn, and will find ourselves putting in 16 hour days 7 days a week through summer. That's not healthy. I would suggest that someone who wants to run everything, should consider having 3 rooms or less for rent. However, it also depends on the amount of involvement the owner wants. We know owners that hire cooks and cleaners and only manage. Meg and I got into this business to be innkeepers, not managers. So we do most things, and look to hire out things we don't love, like cleaning and paying taxes.

How do you deal with check-ins and check-outs?

We define check-in and check-out times in our policies. Industry standard is check out by 11 with a check-in window of 3-6. Guests understand the former, not so much the latter. We've waited up to 2:00 AM for a guest to arrive. It's also not at all uncommon for them to try to check in 3 hours early. We try to accommodate where we can. We've also added late check out and early check-in fees, to discourage bad behavior.

NINETY-FIVE

Hilo Bay Hale Bed and Breakfast

301 Ponahawai St, Hilo, HI 96720

Matthew Potts
Owner

WHAT TIME DO YOU WAKE UP EACH MORNING AND WHAT DOES YOUR schedule look like?

5am wake up to roosters at the farm. One hour of coffee and emails. Leave farm at 6 Drive to Hilo farmers market shop for breakfast. Arrive BNB to start breakfast at 7am. Serve buffet style at 8-9am fir 2-10 guests. Cleaned up kitchen by 10am. Start 4 room cleans. Done by 2pm. In the ocean by noon some days. Back to farm most afternoons.

What is the most rewarding part of the job?

Hearing good reviews. Making people feel well taken care of.

Do you need to be a great cook to run a B&B?

It helps to love what you are doing. It comes through in the details of cooking and finding out what each guest may want or need. Ask them questions about food and how to customize any special requests. Then deliver that with aloha In your heart.

Can one person run a B&B themselves? At what point do you need help?

I have done it myself for months on end. Get help as soon as you can afford to hire or consider a well balanced work trade situation with someone who impresses you with what they bring to the table.

How do you deal with check-ins and check-outs?

I deal with checkins and checkouts very simply. I heave an envelope with their keys fir them and a detailed info sheet in their rooms.

NINETY-SIX

Avalon Bed & Breakfast

1317 Duval Street,
Key West, FL 33040

Yvonne

WHAT TIME DO YOU WAKE UP EACH MORNING AND WHAT DOES YOUR schedule look like?

I am semi retired (only 45 - 50 hours a week these days).

What is the most rewarding part of the job?

The guests. Seeing people come back year after year, watching their families grow. Pre Covid meeting people from all over the world. Pre Covid it was not unusual to have 101 different nationalities staying at the property on any one given night.

Do you need to be a great cook to run a B&B?

No, just creative.

Can one person run a B&B themselves? At what point do you need help?

No. You would never sleep & have no family life. Everyone wants to own a B & B. Most try to sell after 3 years. It is not a retirement job it's a career.

How do you deal with check-ins and check-outs?

As quickly and efficiently as possible. Tempers can be fraught after a long drive through the Keys. Get them to a cool room ASAP and let them unwind.

NINETY-SEVEN

Brewery Gulch Inn

9401 N. Highway 1
Mendocino, CA 95460

Guy Pacurar
Proprietor

- AAA 4-diamond since 2002

- Consistent recognition in Conde Nast, Travel + Leisure and USA Today top lodging properties in the world lists

- Consistent recipient of TripAdvisor's Travelers' Choice Award

- Member of Green Hotels Association

- Member of Audubon Sanctuary program

WHAT TIME DO YOU WAKE UP EACH MORNING AND WHAT DOES YOUR schedule look like?

About 6:30a, but that has nothing to do with the inn and everything to do with having an 8-year old. I am at the inn 5 days a week overseeing the finances, marketing and interacting with guests.

What is the most rewarding part of the job?

Meeting the guests and making new friends.

Do you need to be a great cook to run a B&B?

No, you need to have a great chef. We are fortunate that our price point affords me the luxury of having a culinary staff and a GM.

Can one person run a B&B themselves?

I was told when I first began my search that 1-9 rooms is a hobby and 10+ is a business. We have 11 rooms here and it is a comfortable amount for me. We have the ability to run at 90% year-round, but we hold rooms back and keep our occupancy in the mid-70s. I've found that the trade off on the wear and tear, and the guest experience isn't worth the higher occupancy.

At what point do you need help?

From the day I was born:-) I found that I don't have to know how to do it all, but I have to know how to find good people and set the standard for them to follow. For our 11-room inn, we have a full and part-time staff of 18 people. I know it can be done with less, but for me, my objective wasn't to become wealthy doing this, but to create an experience that stayed with the guest.

How do you deal with check-ins and check-outs?

I'm not sure I understand the question. We have created a contactless check-in option for guests who prefer it, but we find that most people that come to a B&B come for the personalized experience. Few opt for contactless check in.

NINETY-EIGHT

Market Street Inn

220 E Market St
Taylorville, IL 62568-2212

Myrna & Joe Hauser
Innkeepers for 26 years

FROM THE OWNER:

We recently downsized from 10 rooms to only 2 rooms in our carriage house. Our website has been edited to reflect the recent changes. At our age in our late 70's, it is time to slow down. After 26 years of very successful innkeeping, my comments to you are:

Make certain that your website is mobile responsive, so guests can quickly see pics and read reviews. I have heard new guests say that if there are no reviews, then look for an inn with good reviews.

Have your webmaster make on-line reservations available-- guests are in a hurry and really don't want to take to innkeeper, especially after reading our great reviews.

We are blessed with strong corporate clientele--garnered by attending monthly Chamber of Commerce social hours, e.g. Had 33 nights of stay when a new shoe store came to town. Our local hospital places temp staff here. Offer flexible breakfast times

Offer free and robust wi-fi----ours is fiber optic. Also place a smart flat screen TV in each guest room.

Our inn was a member of Select Registry for several years--it was mandatory to hand an annual guide book to each guest. It was interesting how several were not interested in a book saying that we do everything on-line. Our Illinois state association has eliminated the guidebook and does everything on-line. With that in mind, I would suggest that you consider on-line offerings as a priority.

NINETY-NINE

Hawaii's Hidden Hideaway Bed & Breakfast

1369 Mokolea Drive
Kailua, HI 96734

Janice Nielsen

WHAT TIME DO YOU WAKE UP EACH MORNING AND WHAT DOES YOUR schedule look like?

When we are busy, we want to make sure guests have everything they need. Since each of our units are private (entrances, bathrooms, dining areas in the units), we do not necessarily see everyone every day.

What is the most rewarding part of the job?

Meeting the people and becoming close friends with some of them.

Do you need to be a great cook to run a B&B?

NO

Can one person run a B&B themselves?

You can and I have, but you can overdo it by yourself.

At what point do you need help?

One really needs help with cleaning.

How do you deal with check-ins and check-outs?

We have a unique way where guests can check in and out by themselves. This works well since many of our guests are international and arrive at all times of the day and NIGHT.

ONE HUNDRED

Maison de Terre

21704 Uintah Road
Cedaredge CO 81413

Marty and Terrie Watts

**WHAT TIME DO YOU WAKE UP EACH MORNING AND WHAT DOES YOUR
schedule look like?**

We get up between five and six depending on when our guest
would like to eat breakfast. That is usually cleaned up by nine.
After the guest leave several hours of cleaning and iron sheets
follow.

What is the most rewarding part of the job?

The most rewarding part of having a bed and breakfast is
interacting with be wonderful guest that cross our threshold.

Do you need to be a great cook to run a B&B?

Being an excellent cook is certainly important. Since cooking has always been an important part of our lives, we don't really think about the importance of being a great cook; that is something, like having a great house that came with the territory.

Can one person run a B&B themselves? At what point do you need help?

We are a husband and wife partnership. It is nice to have four hands to take care of all of the necessary tasks. We do our own books, website, marketing, taxes, and household chores. We pay outside for Airbnb, Expedia, and a service to manage our reservations.

How do you deal with check-ins and check-outs?

We personally check in our guests. They usually say good-bye when they leave.

ONE HUNDRED ONE

Maria's Creekside B&B

2770 E 46th Ave
Anchorage, Alaska 99507

Robert L Bell

- 9.8 out of 10 on Expedia and 9.6 out of 10 on Booking after
seven years.

WHAT TIME DO YOU WAKE UP EACH MORNING AND WHAT DOES YOUR
schedule look like?

6am. Breakfast prep till 7am. Serve breakfast till 9am. Clean rooms. I help with breakfast prep and leave to operate our retail business. Maria cleans rooms and does laundry.

What is the most rewarding part of the job?

We have met wonderful people from all over the world.

Do you need to be a great cook to run a B&B?

Yep!. That is if you are going to actually serve breakfast. That is Maria's department.

Can one person run a B&B themselves? At what point do you need help?

We have a 3 guestroom B&B. It would be a lot of work for one person. In the winter Maria does most of the work. In the summer we hire help.

How do you deal with check-ins and check-outs?

We use Little Hotelier (Siteminder) channel manager. We used to juggle Booking, Expedia, Airbnb. Without a channel manager it is a mess.

ONE HUNDRED TWO

Bed and Bagels of Tucson

10402 E Glenn St
Tucson, Arizona 85749

WHAT TIME DO YOU WAKE UP EACH MORNING AND WHAT DOES YOUR schedule look like?

I'm both an early bird and a night owl by nature. I'm usually up by 6:30 to let my dog out.

Till Covid hit,, I directed an exercise and memory and language stimulation program for persons with dementia at theTucson Jewish Community Center. The program was "staffed" by University of 'Arizona student interns and volunteers. Plus I attended morning exercise classes 4 days a week. So I tried to serve breakfast by 8 a.m. and, if guests weren't ready, would leave it prepared for my live-in assistant to serve, and clean up after. Since Covid, I serve breakfast at whatever time the guests request.

What is the most rewarding part of the job?

Preparing and serving interesting breakfasts tor guests and swapping travel stories with them. Helping them make the best use of their time in Tucson by suggesting activities and places to visit. I know all the pet friendly places.

Do you need to be a great cook to run a B&B?

My mother used to say,"if you can read, you can cook!" Most guests don't stay longer than 3 or 4 days. I have 3 or 4 favorite breakfasts that I use consistently and half a dozen others that I trot out for longer term guests. I offer juice, a small fruit plate, a hot or cold entree, a bread product, and a cake or pastry and coffee or tea. I take advantage of prepared products and use them in different ways. I'll serve store-bought tamales with scrambled eggs. salsa, and a special sausage, or frozen cheese blintzes in a soufflé with homemade blueberry or strawberry sauce, or, slices of polenta (available in a fast sausage like roll) in individual ramekins as the base for individual baked egg, cheese, capers, and sometimes sliced tomato and lox casseroles. I try to vary the fruit offering and offer yogurt or a sour cream/maple syrup or orange juice topping. I offer whole strawberry and sliced bananas with a dollop of sour cream and a small mound of brown sugar for dipping. Another favorite combo is alternating slices of orange and kiwi, with aside of a contrasting fruit such as black grapes, blueberries or blackberries. Apples can be served sliced with peanut butter and caramel dips or in a Waldorf salad. Fresh pineapple is always available. Of course, in summer, lots more are available.Occasionally, I'll make smoothies out of a banana, some other fruit if available, yogurt, fruit juice, and crushed ice. I place homemade chocolate chip cookies (and a biscuit or jerky treat for dogs) in rooms for guests on arrival. (I freeze balls of made-ahead cookie dough and bake as needed.)

In summer, there's lots to choose from. Pink grapefruit segments in large jars or individual servings are available at supermarkets. I add cinnamon to the coffee grounds when I brew Guests seem to like it. Most supermarkets now carry large boxes of non-refrigerated individual dairy and non-dairy creamers in individual packaging. I keep those on hand. I also have an array of teas - with and without caffeine and an electric teapot available for "self-service.

Can one person run a B&B themselves? At what point do you need help?

It's possible, not recommended, m if you have any kind of a life! I have as large room which I offer rent free in exchange for chores. In the 25 years I've been running Bed and Bagels, I've had a terrific series of people in this role, some with pets of their own, several of whom have remained trusted friends after they've moved on.

How do you deal with check-ins and check-outs?

No set time. I ask for an estimated time of arrival when the guest books and ask them to call when they're about an hour away. If I or my assistant aren't going to be there when they come, I tell them where the key and their room is and to make themselves at home my dog is confined to a gated family room and is friendly to visitors; If there's no incoming guests, I let guests stay most of

the day on their "check out day, possibly asking them to vacate
the bedroom bu continue to enjoy the property.

ONE HUNDRED THREE

Sweet Dreams B&B

14829 Morrison Street
Sherman Oaks, CA, 91403

Amy Ram
Owner/Innkeeper

- Official CABBI Associate

- Top performer on TripAdvisor and have received the TripAdvisor Certificate of Excellence 5 years in a row

---

WHAT IS THE MOST REWARDING PART OF THE JOB?

The most rewarding part of this is getting to meet all types of people from the most amazing walks of life. Every guest has a fun or crazy story!

Do you need to be a great cook to run a B&B?

Absolutely not! At the very minimum you should be provided basic motel continental breakfast foods. Cereal, oatmeal, bagels, coffee -- these items don't need professional hands! Having home cooked breakfast is always preferred however. There is nothing like waking up to a fresh breakfast that smells like mom cooked it!

Can one person run a B&B themselves? At what point do you need help?

One person can absolutely run a B&B by themselves, but it would take a lot of time. I like to get help in the places where I am not strong at, so I have someone that helps manage.

How do you deal with check-ins and check-outs?

I have always been very lenient when it comes to check-in and check-out. Especially when coronavirus became high risk, I wanted to ensure that people could access their room without having to interact with anyone. Prior to COVID I would let the guests into their room and provide their key, answer any questions, and show them the property over tea or coffee.

ONE HUNDRED FOUR

Whispering Winds Retreat B&B

65095 Lingonberry Rd
Ninilchik, Alaska 99639

Fred Eggert

WHAT TIME DO YOU WAKE UP EACH MORNING AND WHAT DOES YOUR schedule look like?

Varies depending on guest needs for the day. Sometimes at 3am, usually by 5am. After breakfast is served and cleaning for the day completed, schedule is wide open.

What is the most rewarding part of the job?

Seeing a smile on my customers face because they are enjoying their stay

Do you need to be a great cook to run a B&B?

No. We offer simple breakfast, with as much as possible made from scratch.

Can one person run a B&B themselves?

Yes, but I wouldn't want to.

At what point do you need help?

Cleaning for the next guest

How do you deal with check-ins and check-outs?

Check-in is a meet and greet with payment. Check-out, the guest simply leaves.

ONE HUNDRED FIVE

Brigitte's Bavarian Bed und Breakfast

59800 Tern Court, Box 2391
Homer, Alaska 99603

Willie und Brigitte Suter

**WHAT TIME DO YOU WAKE UP EACH MORNING AND WHAT DOES YOUR
schedule look like?**

Accommodating guests is *Numero Uno* - the fishermen start
early, might be served accordingly or take food with them onto
the boat. Most guests are moving about during the day,
exploring.

What is the most rewarding part of the job?

Rewards come in all kinds of colors: breakfast to their liking, good sleep on a firm mattress, a yard to their liking, sitting around the fire-place, relaxing, communicating their good feelings towards the hosts - ambience

---

Do you need to be a great cook to run a B&B?

Just do a good job, honest food, no junk or cutting corners [to save money] Spend time to prepare/cook food, treat them all like family.

Can one person run a B&B themselves? At what point do you need help?

Don't know how this would/could work.

How do you deal with check-ins and check-outs?

Just do it
